W9-BSO-193

PASSAGES ABOUT EARTH

Also by William Irwin Thompson

The Imagination of an Insurrection: Dublin, Easter 1916

At the Edge of History

A LINDISFARNE BOOK

PASSAGES ABOUT EARTH

An Exploration of the New Planetary Culture

William Irwin Thompson

HARPER & ROW, PUBLISHERS

New York, Evanston, San Francisco, London

Grateful acknowledgment is hereby made to the following publishers for use of material under copyright. For lines from T. S. Eliot's "Little Gidding" and "Burnt Norton" in *Four Quartets* from *Collected Poems, 1909–1962* (copyright, 1943), Harcourt Brace Jovanovich. For lines from William Butler Yeats's "Lapis Lazuli" and "Meditations in Time of Civil War" from *The Collected Poems of W. B. Yeats* (copyright, 1934; renewed by Bertha Georgie Yeats, 1962), The Macmillan Company. For lines from William Butler Yeats's *A Full Moon in March* from *The Collected Plays of W. B. Yeats* (copyright, 1934; renewed by Bertha Georgie Yeats, 1962), The Macmillan Company.

Chapter One, "The Lift-Off Limits," appeared in somewhat different form on the Op Ed page of the *New York Times*, January 1, 1973. Copyright © 1973 by The New York Times Company. Reprinted by permission. Earlier versions of other chapters first appeared as essays published in *Harper's Magazine*.

FIRST EDITION

LIBRARY OF CONGRESS CATALOG CARD NUMBER: 73–14298

STANDARD BOOK NUMBER: 0–06–014272–3

Designed by Sidney Feinberg

Dedicated to the memory of my father,
Chester Andrew Thompson, and to the future
of his grandchildren, Evan and Hilary

Contents

PASSAGES ABOUT EARTH

The Lift-off Limits

It was the night of the last rocket to the moon, and on that crowded day in December an era came to its final point. The event was not science, it was mythology. Across the surface of the lagoon, the apparition cast great beams of light up into the sky and down upon the face of the waters. With the V in the sky reflected in the water, the St. Andrew's Cross of the rocket stood out like an icon against the night. Behind the rocket to the north a tropical storm retreated with bolts of lightning that seemed like the boasting threats of a small boy backing away from a fight.

I sat at the very edge of the lagoon, where a dolphin swam back and forth and occasionally leaped up to catch a sight of the illumination. Did it with its brain larger than a man's know what we were up to; had it come as spy or witness to keep nightwatch on our attempt to escape? To my right Carl Sagan beeped to the dolphin in a stab at intraterrestrial speech, and then returned to unfamiliar thoughts in a more familiar English. He spoke of life on Mars, of a background radiation in space that was leftover starlight from a *future* universe: future because its time flowed in a direction opposite to ours. I thought of Yeats's twin interpenetrating gyres and wondered why we should think of it as future at all; perhaps that other universe was right here in this now—a *Doppelgänger* universe in which "each lived the other's death, died the other's life." And always, as the countdown was delayed hour after hour, the rocket stood as a reminder that thoughts of rockets to the moon were once as fantastic as Sagan's present speculations. In 1600 Giordano Bruno was burned at the stake for the following heresy:

> I hold the universe to be infinite, as being the effect of infinite divine power and goodness, of which any finite world would have been unworthy. Hence I have declared infinite worlds to exist beside this our Earth; I hold with Pythagoras that the Earth is a star like all the others which are infinite, and that all these numberless worlds are a whole in infinite space, which is the true universe.

Now Sagan shared these thoughts safely with thousands. And perhaps, just as another universe was leftover starlight in ours, so Bruno was slipping out of his time into that night. The illuminated rocket and the burning stake stood out as two poles of scientific thought around which an inhuman darkness gathered.

What a few men had experienced in imagination, thousands now were to see. Apollo 17 was not the lonely frontier of human exploration; it was not the forward guard, but the collective center, the wake of Bruno whose waves now tossed us about 372 years after his death. A socialization of the imagination, the rocket was at once an institution and a ritual. Just as a religious ceremony brought exaltation to those who did not have visions of the face of God, so now technology would bring excitement to those who did not have visions of universal science. Small wonder that all the rockets had the names of mythological deities.

And nothing except a religious experience could surpass the

elevation of that host. We had all been prepared for spectacle; but when the engines ignited, the night went away, and the force of the rocket entered my body. There was no heavy blast that hurt my ears; instead, the engines beat in a subtler rhythm that went directly and physically into the chambers of the heart and made all the valves stammer in astonishment. If it weren't for the joy and exhilaration of the crowd, I would have wondered if my heart would stop. But as I felt my heart continue with the progress of the rocket in the sky, I threw away anxiety and leaped up with the others in the sheer joy of knowing that men were turning tables on the heavens and riding that comet out of earth.

When the second stage ignited, the breath of the crowd released itself in sympathy with the rocket's bright exhaust. Now there was no doubt; they were on their way. The rocket's escape from earth was a celebration; and if some scoffed that these were our pyramids, then at least these perishable monuments truly expressed us: a people with little history but enormous energy. Call that first rocket falling to the sea an artifact, and on it write what anonymous stonemasons inscribed on medieval cathedrals: "Adam made me."

For all the talk of the dehumanization of technology, nowhere was human emotion more nakedly expressed. The faces of the scientists were the faces of men who had witnessed the Transfiguration on the Mount. If science makes the unknown familiar, and if art makes the familiar strange and wonderfully new, then this recovery of wonder was not *Wissenschaft*, but *Wissenkunst*. And this is the new stage in human culture we have reached, a planetary society containing more bits of information than the mind can stand, but holding enough space for the spirit to soar.

Long ago in the tribal society of Marx's primitive communism, all knowledge was art. Tools were pieces of sculpture and cave paintings were symbols through which man gained the balance with nature. The very first miniaturization of the universe, the painted cave was an alphabet of symbols, an alphabet that was to begin as scratches on a rock but end as pulses on a tape.

After domesticating animals and plants, man went on to domesticate man. It was to be called civilization, but it was also slavery. A new technology separated itself from the old neolithic religion, and a new civilized, literate elite separated itself from the illiterate tribes. Now art became a celebration of power and glory, but since man had only recently emerged from nature's dominance, it was a nervous whistling in the dark; underneath the celebration of glory remained the awareness of death. Here in the great foundations of Western literature, the *Gilgamesh* and the *Iliad*, man's art celebrated the pursuit of excellence (*areté*) and all the contradictions contained in that quest.

For thousands of years man's culture lingered at this agricultural, civilizational level; but then in Great Britain toward the end of the eighteenth century, human culture took another quantum leap. The Industrial Revolution brought in a whole new technology, and with it a whole new art. The art was no longer a celebration of the glory of kings and princes, but the autobiography of the middle classes. It was a story of personal, individual movement in time and space: from rags to riches, from the country to the city and back again. This was an art about the pursuit of independence and the contradictions contained in that freedom. Underneath the pursuit of wealth, power, and fame, and underneath the search for absolute autonomy, was the individual man confronting his solitude. As it had in the agricultural revolution, so in the Industrial Revolution did technology separate itself from the old religious world view. The world was split in two: the hard, masculine, and objective world of machines; and the soft, feminine, and subjective world of emotions. Art, if it was to justify its existence in a world of "real things," had to copy things; mimesis was what art was all about, and the novel grew to replace the epic as the supreme form.

Now we are taking another quantum leap in human culture. Marx would call it socialism; Boulding would call it post-civilization; and McLuhan would call it the electronic return to the tribe. The old art of the novel falls behind, for now reality itself becomes the work of art, and the lift-off of a rocket becomes a concert. And so the cycle spins around, as Vico, Marx, and McLuhan knew it would. In primitive communism, art was knowledge; in electronic socialism, it is knowledge itself that becomes the work of art. In a world in which men write thousands of books and one million scientific papers a year, the mythic *bricoleur* is the man who plays with all that information and hears a music inside the noise.

When most men were hunters, the cave painters gave a form to the culture. They did not simply make a copy of the hunt after it was over; they created the hunt that was to be and directed men through a forest of symbols in the new dimensions of mind-and-nature. Now that most men are students in our informational society, the *Wissenkunstler* does not simply make a copy of the day in the life of a banker or a soldier; he moves out of the cultural reality of art and science into "A Separate Reality" in which figure and ground are reversed and all the old facts fall into new and often alien forms of consciousness. In the old modern era, science was "objective" and art was "subjective"; but now the attraction of opposites has brought them together and neither science nor art is where it used to be.

On looking at the archaic Apollo, Rilke said to himself: "Du musst Dein Leben ändern"—You must make your life over." So it is on looking at Apollo 17. For those astronauts who have looked on the earth from space, the command has been literally taken to heart as they felt their consciousness being transformed to behold God making all things new. Perhaps this transformation of consciousness, this new aesthetic high in man's culture, is the strongest argument in favor of manned space flight. Had we merely sent out efficient instruments of measurement, we would have expanded our technology while constricting our culture. The machines would literally encircle man and inevitably tighten the space around him. Now that we have sent out man to surround his machines, we have affirmed that technology is still only a part of culture. We have also affirmed that the culture of America is still significantly different from that of the Soviet Union. The Russian decision in favor of mechanized space flight illustrates the iron lock dialectical materialism has on their archaic industrial culture. Had the materialists at home convinced us that the money for manned space flight should be spent on more pressing problems, they would also have convinced us that it should go to the experts in the field of behavioral problems, and a psychological inner-space program would have arisen under the direction of men like Harvard's behavioral psychologist B. F. Skinner or Yale's psychosurgeon José M. Delgado. Under the misguided notion that we had to use our technology to solve our problems here on earth, we would have robbed ourselves of the chance to become more than the identity dictated to us by our problems. When you see a man or a society as only a problem to be solved, you dehumanize that man and reduce that society to an abstract system. Were we to give the equivalent of a space program to Dr. Delgado (and he has indeed asked for just such a thing), we would simply turn the whole country into a state hospital of the worst kind. If it has done nothing else, the space program has saved us from that fate. Now that the space program is being discontinued, we can rightfully begin to be afraid.

Whether through luck or divine guidance, America has

taken one giant step toward humanizing its technology. Through an imaginative expansion of the spirit beyond the the clever ironies and sophistications of the New York intelligentsia, the Southern and Midwestern hicks and the West Coast freaks have brought technology down to size. While the intellectuals complained about the dehumanization brought on by machines and sought, out of a love for their afflictions, to make psychotherapy into a way of life, the religious hicks pricked the sky with a rocket, letting all the hot air out and all the heavenly vibrations in. It was a rerun of American history, for the New York intellectuals had turned toward Europe, while the South, Midwest, and West Coast had turned toward the new wilderness. And just as once the European went into the American wilderness and came out as a new archetypal hero, a Natty Bumppo or a Daniel Boone, so now a new archetypal hero seems to be emerging from space. According to *Time* reporter Leo Janos, many of the astronauts have found the journey into space to be a conversion experience. Thus the man of the new wilderness is not a robot-like technician, but another Natty Bumppo leading civilization back to the Indians. Rusty Schweikart is a follower of the Maharishi's Transcendental Meditation, and Edgar Mitchell is now doing research into psychic healing, ESP, psychokinesis, and astral projection. Interestingly enough, C. S. Lewis prophesied just such a strange turn over thirty years ago. In his theological science fiction novel, *Out of the Silent Planet*, Lewis describes the surprise of the first space voyager who discovers that space is not a void, but a divine plenum. Men are prisoners of war in an enemy territory that shuts out all the vibrations of heaven, but all those who break out of this, the devil's planet soon regain their cosmic orientation.

This recovery of our lost cosmic orientation will probably prove to be more historically significant than the design of the Saturn V rocket. One could not help but feel in the blaze of Apollo 17 that there was a sunset-effect to this technology of rockets. And certainly the knowledge that this was to be the last of the Apollos gave the crowd the sharp and poignant sense of an ending. Although many took the feelings of exaltation on that night to be demands for the continuation of the Apollo project, I did not. Apollo 17 was a consummation, but the consummation often occurs when its opposite movement has just begun. The year the most advanced horseshoe was designed was the year the automobile was invented; the year the *Edinburgh Review* published the last word on catastrophist geology was the year Lyell published his classic work on uniformitarianism. Apollo 17 turned the night into day, but elsewhere smaller lights are going on as men begin to discover the relationship between human consciousness and plants at the Backster Institute, between enzyme change and faith healing at the Human Dimensions Institute, and between mind and matter in psychokinesis at the Stanford Research Institute. The space program was an important scaffolding, but once the building of the new culture is up, we no longer need the scaffolding. The new space shuttle should not be a polluting rocket, but an elegant antigravity device; the new source of power should not be the controlled hydrogen bombs of thermonuclear fusion, but a gentler respiration of the sun. To develop these new transformations we will need more than government funds for basic research; we will need the imagination and spirit with which to experience a new kind of science. There is much to be done in terms of superconductors, antigravity, the solar wind, and the understanding of the subtler forces that bind the single-quantum states of organisms. To spend a fortune on rockets now would be the same as spending a fortune on dirigibles in 1916. There are other forms of space travel to be invented, and these forms are more likely to spring from the paradigm emerging in the new Pythagorean science than from the hardware and bureaucracy of the old Archimedean technology. There is new information coming in, and the more the mass of our total information expands to infinity, the more our consciousness must quicken to the speed of light.

Walking Out On the University

How much easier it would be if there were only visible events to describe rather than invisible transformations to explain, if I could tell you a story. You would think an historian would be good at that, but that's just the problem: history. How can an historian deal with something larger than history, with a transformation of culture so large that it isn't an event any more?

Once when I was walking along the rocky seashore of Malta, the enormity of the scale of historical measurement broke in upon me. It was low tide and the strange mustard-colored rocks were full of pools then quite distant from the sea. As I looked at the forms of life, I wondered how it must seem to swim in a pool where once one had had the sea. And then the shallows became the earth and I thought of how we were once a planet washed over by great cosmic tides, and then the tide drew back and took with it all the great creatures of the deep, and we were left stranded to swim in our puddles and speak of the greatness of man.

It is a long time between tides. The Maya with their mythological calendar for measuring historical time would say that the tide went out in 3113 B.C. and will not return until midnight of Christmas Eve in the year 2011. Man has had time enough to forget about the sea and make a universe of a crevice in a rock. But now you can feel the waters lift and stir; new currents are coming in, but for those of us in the universities who cannot stand the flooding of our academic boundaries and definitions, there will be terror as the mythical future becomes confused with the mythical past. Looking at the pool at my feet, I sensed the sea at my back and climbed up to the comfort of the higher rocks.

Something has already happened, something so vast that all our social-science descriptions of man cannot add up to it. The record of civilization is over, and like a record at its end, it keeps going on with the noise of a needle stuck in its rut: the revolution of the workers, the protest of the young, the new creations of the avant-garde, the rise of new forms of sexual liberation, the appearance of new religions. This side of history is over, and on the other side is myth.

The historian can sit in the library and do research, but the mythographer travels in his ideas through books, and space, and time; any book casually taken off the library shelf is likely to leave a hole through which another reality beckons. Thus research into civilization can become *the* search for a new civilization. The more books I read in order to write *At the Edge of History*, the larger the hole became, until finally I could walk through to look at history from the other side. I knew when I walked through that hole in the university to begin the wandering around the world in search of Lindisfarne that I would not come back, and yet the external traveling did not cover as great a distance as the steps I had to take inside myself to let go of the comfortable structures of the old culture. As an historian in a university I was merely marking time, and when I realized that *I* could not live in a new civilization *and* the university, any more than I could live in the water and still be dry, I struggled onto the shore with the slow and painful movements of a lungfish forcing his old fins to become new legs.

But it was not all personal, for everywhere around me I could see the signs of an historical era coming to an end. A fine finish to Western civilization shone out on the bright glass buildings of the modern state university. What was hidden in all the camouflage of tradition at Oxford or Princeton, and only sensed in fleeting moments of inattention in common rooms and faculty clubs, was brazenly expressed in the office-building architecture of the universities of the post-industrial state. Just a few years ago great buildings were dedicated with speeches that celebrated a new age of triumphant rationality created by enlightened investment in higher education. With the best intentions of demonstrating the high level of modern society made secure by the new management sciences, governments spent lavish funds on building citadels of progress with wall-to-wall carpets and occasional pieces of art.

Now these same buildings are slums where sullen bodies sprawl along the floor and pass a joint among themselves. Like Indians on a reservation or the poor in public housing, these students treat their physical surroundings with a contempt for the facile condescension built into the forms of their incarceration. They put out their cigarettes in the carpets, steal the paintings from the walls, strew their trash everywhere, bring their barking dogs into the lectures, and leave their old condoms in the elevators of the coeducational dorms. If the students must study, they cut out the assigned section of the book from the reserve room in the library, or, if the book is naïvely left in the open stacks, they steal it altogether. If that is too much trouble, then they buy a term paper from a company organized for the purpose. With four-track stereo minds, they pile sound on sound, and listen to portable TVs while they read, hold rock concerts in the academic halls, and talk and walk about during the lectures.

Navahos speeding in a Ford pickup and slinging beer cans out the window onto the Arizona mesa could not show more contempt for the irrelevance of their traditions than do these denizens of the modern Youth Reservation.

These are the children of the suburbs, who have been institutionalized in schools all their lives. They almost always obey, but they take out their repressed rebellion in acts of trivial revolt like the trashing of the campus, for in garbage they sense the entropic state of our civilization. What the city fathers deny with their buildings, the kids affirm with their trash. Without the courage to drop out or the will to suffer their freedom, the ones who remain institutionalized take a compensatory pride in acts of bourgeois petty thievery and think that in "ripping off" a book from the student bookstore they have committed an act of existential affirmation in the face of the Establishment. Closed within a tightening space, ecologically and socially, they move through a socialized culture in which institutions like the school, the detention center, and public housing are all of a piece. There are no tramp steamers left, no Foreign Legions or Lincoln Brigades. Their adventurous brothers and sisters may have struck out to see the world of Youth Culture in chartered jets: to smoke hash in Marrakech, to shoot smack in Istanbul, and to drop acid in Katmandu; but history has left these obedient children behind in an eroticized bureaucracy. And yet they do not make love to one another; they "ball." They no longer take LSD to find the face of God; they take coke to intensify their private orgasms and downers to make the vanishing music last.

This is the paradoxical university of the students: a Dionysian bureaucracy. The university of the faculty is its mirror-image: an Apollonian irrationality. All is order and methodology. As soon as consciousness senses a threat, an academic methodology breaks it down in pieces so that the whole problem cannot be seen. Utterly engrossed in the details of committee work, these specialists could pluck hairs from the face of terror and never have to look it in the eye. Forced to spend more of their lives in committees than in the classroom or library, these teachers are taught how to become "managers of a learning system." In each committee a crisis comes regularly along to convince the professor of his new importance in the wider sphere of public affairs. He no longer notices that the internal mimeographed material from all his committees weighs up to fifty pounds a year. He succumbs to his responsibilities, but he takes the students down with him, for now they, too, are allowed to serve on committees, to become responsible members of the academic community.

The contemporary university with its socialized education is, as the founding president of York University, Murray Ross, has said, "a large public corporation." Its purpose is, therefore, to teach people how to live in a large public corporation, and this can be done as well in a committee as in a classroom. In fact, as committees begin to dominate the life of a university, the atmosphere of the classroom changes from one of a teacher with his students to one of a committee chairman with a team of consultants. The role of an educational bureaucracy is to educate people to bureaucracy, and this can be done as well in a course in humanities as in one in business administration. If one controls the structure, he can afford to allow a liberal amount of play in the content. The more that alien subjects like mysticism, revolution, or sexuality can be brought into the structures of curricular behavior determined by educational management, the more these structures prove their power over just those areas of experience that might subvert them.

The call for reform from within thus becomes one of the cleverest devices to preserve the structure. Reformers fancy that by opening up the curriculum to subjects that seem relevant to youth, such as poverty, abortion, or gay liberation, they will create a healthy university; but all they really will be doing is offering Sociology 100, 101, 102, 103. The culture of the university remains the same.

And the culture will remain the same until the problem is seen as a whole. The problem as a whole is that our institutions are no longer in sync with the pattern of human growth through time. We think that time is a line that moves from bad to better, from poverty to progress, from ignorance to knowledge, from grades 1 to 20. The point of the line is to develop an identity through a function and then maintain that function for as "long" as possible. Any deviation from the line is deviant behavior. The sins of the fathers are passed on to the sons, and this unfortunate patrimony is our inheritance from the industrial era.

Before the Industrial Revolution, children worked with their parents and relatives on the farm. They did not have to be flattered as being responsible members of the community, for it would never have occurred to anyone to consider them anything else. But when the factories began to replace cottage industries, the parents became collectivized in the new institution, and so it was thought only natural that the children should be too. But the younger members of the human species did not take to industrialization so readily; the factory literally became a Procrustean bed, and as the children began to lose eye and limb from their encounter with the machines, it became obvious that they did not fit in the new institution of the factory. And so a new institution was created, the public school, and the collectivization of the parents was matched in the collectivization of the children.

The public school in America was more powerful than its counterpart in Great Britain. Since we were a nation of immigrants, the central task of the school was Americanization. Whatever the teacher may have said about the three R's, she was basically saying: "Your parents have an accent; I don't. If you want to belong to America, you must reject your parents and come to me." Like an apparitional Statue of Liberty, the public school teacher held an illusory torch of learning aloft and summoned all the waifs to her side. She took the children away from their parents, just as America took the immigrants away from Europe. The children learned their lessons well; they Anglicized their names and moved into education and teaching as the most immediately open vehicle of upward mobility—and power, the power to become matriarchal statues of liberty themselves. In the age of print, when big cities and big books contained what civilization had to offer, the system went on unchallenged. But by the age of television the media became a more effective means of Americanization. The educational system that had worked on the Jews or the Irish could no longer work on the blacks; and when Jewish teachers in New York tried to take black children away from their parents exactly in the way they had been taken from theirs, they were shocked to encounter a violent affirmation of negritude. The encounter was an important one, for the power of education had become too great; while claiming to be the protector of liberty in a democracy, the educational system had slowly grown into a center for the distribution of tranquilizers and behavioral modification. The public school system, which had been created to put muscle into democracy, ended up by becoming the closing fingers of the long arm of the state.

When education became big business, it joined up with the union of big business and big government; in all large corporations, public or private, the central feature of behavior is obedience to corporate routines. The lines of desks matched the production line, and time was taken up in progress through grades. From the cradle to the grave, from rags to riches, the new man had to make his way on down the line. Of course, it didn't work very well, but then agricultural civilization hadn't worked very well either. It could have gone on for thousands of years, just as agricultural civilization had, but then something remarkable happened. Industrial civilization came to an end. Daniel Bell would give one reason, McLuhan another, but, whether because of automation or the electronic media, students began to revolt or drop out and Swedish auto workers began to refuse the "chimpanzee work" of the production line.

What was happening was that all the lines of industrial culture were breaking up; people were "making waves" again. The natural life rhythms of Homo Sapiens were reasserting themselves after two centuries of hibernation in the iron winter of the industrial era. Teenagers began dropping out of school; middle-aged men took dramatic turns into whole new careers; and housewives walked out of the kitchen with as much religious yearning as the Lord Gautama had when he walked out of the nursery of his sleeping infant.

If one stays inside a kitchen, a school, or a corporation, then what is happening looks terrible and anarchic: all civilization is breaking down. But if one moves outside, he can see that on the other side of the social uterine wall there is sunlight and space in which to breathe and move, and that, in fact, after a few cries of fear, it is all rather wonderful. There is more pulse to this new life, and if it moves in alternating waves, that does not mean that it lacks an overall sense of direction. As creatures begin to take their own time to move *with* life rather than *through* life, we can begin to see that there is a whole new rhythm to the way the pageant unfolds itself.

No longer is there one single identity to man, the functionary; instead, there are now two gods within the self that pulse in a cycle alternating between Homo Ludens, the being of play, and Homo Faber, the doer of work. In the first cycle one experiences a period of creative expansion; in the other, a period of consolidation into form. Each life is unique, and yet each life has a universal pattern, just as all snow is white, but each flake is a different crystal.

As one looks at the procession of individual lives around him, an overall pattern begins to emerge. There is the straight line of institutional clock-time going from the nursery to the nursing home, but pulsing under and over it is the wave of human life-time. The following outline of the alternating waves of life-time should be seen not as a literal description but as a musical staff which shows us how the relationships *work* so that we may learn how to *play*.

Ages 1 to 7 (Homo Ludens)

In the first seven years of life the major project is to master the body and the heart. The child grows through play with his body and his parents; he *feels* his way toward self-mastery through the richly supportive emotional environment of the family.

Ages 7 to 14 (Homo Faber)

At the traditional age of reason, Piaget has confirmed that a profound change takes place. The child loses his emotionally based egocentrism and begins to take a more objective interest in the world. He moves to the mastery of the mind and a delight in the gathering of facts: "How fast can a cheetah run? Can a peregrine falcon fly faster than a cheetah can run? What is the tallest mountain in the world? Who has the most goals in the NHL?" From the secure base of the emotional love of the family, and from the secure base of his own mastery of the body and the native language, he begins to range out from the close and intimate "sexual" relationships in the Oedipal stage into the period Freud described as latency.

Ages 14 to 21 (Homo Ludens)

From the ages of seven to fourteen, when they delight in collecting objects and facts, children should be in school; but by the time of their teens they should be released from school, and in good Maoist fashion sent out to work and play in rural communes. At fourteen the individual begins to experience a new phase of creative expansion; it is what Freud called the period of "the return of the repressed." Now the youth must struggle once again to master the body and the heart, but this time it is the sexually developed body that he must master. Along with the explosions of puberty comes an explosion of new emotions and tenderness. The mode of being shifts from the apparent toughness of the fact-gatherer to a softer and more "feely" approach to all ideas. To try to contain people in schools at this stage of life is to do violence to their whole nature. They need to grow and develop through emotional and physical activities, not through sitting in libraries trying to understand the passionate abstractions of older people. It was in a clumsy recognition of this phase that high schools and colleges were often excuses for football teams, but in the old aggressive and competitive industrial culture there was never a full recognition of all the qualities of adolescence. Adolescents need to grow through sexual discovery, emotional bonding, music, poetry, work, and dance: in short, through play in the truest cultural sense of the word. If human beings are kept in schools during this stage, they will simply convert them into nurseries of show-and-tell. Asked for intellectual papers, they will simply turn in collages, finger paintings, or seven blank pages as a Zen statement. Compressed into a space that forces them to explode, they need to be given an open space which allows them to explore. We do not have to ship them off to a seven-year summer camp. Instead, following the wisdom of the Chinese, we can give them work full of high ideals and new cultural purposes: not the army but such independent cultural centers as Paolo Soleri's Arcosanti.

Ages 21 to 28 (Homo Faber)

After a period of physical and emotional growth through feeling, one begins to surfeit on "feely" approaches to ideas and begins to hunger for what Yeats called "the mastery of what is difficult." All university teachers that I have talked to about the problems of youth culture will readily admit that the best students are those who have dropped out and later returned to college. I first noticed this difference when I had students of different ages in a small seminar. The younger students couldn't care less about Yeats as Yeats; they looked upon the poems as Rorschachs for their own inner workings. The older students were very impatient with the younger ones. They were tired of looking into a mirror and wanted to break out of the closet of their own emotions; they wanted to learn how to read a difficult text and see what Yeats had in mind. There is no question at all in my mind but that well over half the problems of our universities would be solved if we adjusted them to the right age group, opened them up to become resource centers like public libraries, and allowed people to come in at various levels. If people were allowed to have a natural growth from fourteen to twenty-one, then they would not have to endure a delayed adolescence at twenty-four. Students who have gone directly from high school to college are inevitably in a state of emotional frustration. If they have gone to graduate school straight after college, then they are in a state of suspended rage from the suppression of their human natures.

Half of our student protest in the sixties was just such a natural outcome of our unnatural totalizing of education from kindergarten to the Ph.D. Its lack of a true political source was evidenced at Kent State. When the Right Wing obliged the revolutionaries by shooting innocent students, and thus giving them a perfect chance for precipitating a condition of civil war, the student revolutionaries demonstrated that they were more students than revolutionaries. The era of mass student protest came to an end and the students cried, in their own words: "Don't shoot; we are your children." If people were given a full and rich period of development from fourteen to twenty-one, then by twenty-one they would be hungry to follow that period of creative expansion with a period of consolidation into form. Then they would be ready for the civilized rigors of university or professional school; then they could respect and follow traditions without trying to pervert them into caricatures of learning. In a healthy culture people could proceed smoothly from B.A. to Ph.D., LL.B., or M.D. in the period from twenty-one to twenty-eight.

28 to 35 (Homo Ludens)

After a period of training and work comes the joy of the performance of one's skill in a profession. In this period of life one integrates mastery of body, mind, and heart into a new unity of being. The age of thirty-five divides life into what Jungians call the first and the second halves of life. The first half is the period of self-formation; the second half is the period of self-realization. The period from twenty-eight to thirty-five is the age of the career. Here one *is* a lawyer, doctor, teacher, or businessman.

For a woman the pattern is, of course, different, depending on when or if she chooses to enter into the child-bearing stage of life. For those women who choose to bear children, it would seem that the fourteen-year period from twenty-one to thirty-five would be the most likely one. In a postinstitutional culture, cultural centers like universities and professional schools would be open. Now they are often closed and will take only the young who apply directly after high school and refuse to take older or part-time students. Many law and medical schools, for example, insolently refuse to take part-time students because they might ruin the club by filling it up with "housewives." In a healthy culture, however, fathers could go to university along with mothers, and each could help the other in balancing classes and child care. Or, in a different pattern, women could stay home while their children were young and then return to school or work at a later stage.

35 to 49 (Homo Faber)

In the second half of life, when the period of the formation of the self has resulted in the achievement of a unity of body, mind, and heart, the alternating seven-year cycle lengthens to one of fourteen years.[1] After the period of the seven-year performance of one's career, a new restlessness begins to appear in middle life. For many individuals this restlessness will result in a dramatic shift in which they begin a whole new career. Businessmen will become teachers; housewives will go off to law school or decide to get Ph.D.s. Most people, however, are still mentally living in an industrial culture, and so they have difficulty in identifying the source of their restlessness, because they feel that at their established age there should be no reason for it. Unable to find the source, they often make only subtle shifts. Realizing that they are becoming tired of laboratory science or classroom teaching, they may shift into administration (a field much more suited to Homo Faber than Homo Ludens) without admitting to themselves that they are no longer really scientists or teachers.

In business this restlessness may come on at the point of

the satisfaction of one's ambition: after one has the right car, the right house, the right job, he begins to wonder if this is what it was all about. The lure of affluence may lose its force and the person may become more interested in politics or power. Before, power was seen as something one needed in order to get the things he wanted; but at this stage of life power becomes desired for its own sake. At its best, this stage of life is not so much one of the joyous performance of skill as the stage of responsibility, of mastery of institutions, of leadership. This is the time when one builds the structures in which others can joyously perform their skills; it is the time of the dean, the administrator, the politician. It is the age of power, when the individual comes into the fullness of his own powers.

49 to 63 (Homo Ludens)

But power is not meant to last forever. If one has become locked into power in the previous stage, then this new phase of life comes to deliver man from that prison. For those who have repressed too much of their physical and emotional natures, this stage is often a painful confrontation with aging and death. Often a very real heart attack can come to remind the powerful man that he has killed his heart and it now threatens to return the favor. In this new phase there is once again a call to master the body and the emotions. It is for people at this stage of life that the Esalen techniques of *Gestalt* and encounter can be effective forms of deliverance. Or the threat of death itself may bring on a religious awakening, and the individual may pull back from the public exercise of power into a new privacy and concern for the self.

This concern for the self could become a morbid and depressive state in which the individual loses all touch with

life, but in the natural scheme of things this period is also
the time of grandparenthood. And so the individual is brought
back in touch with life and returns to the heart and the body
in a religious association with the continuity of human time
through the generations. The phase thus becomes a period
of creative expansion, of broadening horizons and outlooks
beyond the drive for power. Out of the confrontation with
aging and death, a fuller and deeper humanity can emerge.
Man can see the play of life and once again become Man the
Player. When such an individual returns to the conditions
of the mind and social institutions, he brings to them a new
spiritual force. At this stage of life, as Homo Ludens, with
comedy in one eye and tragedy in the other, the person is
ready to be entrusted with the custodianship of the institutions themselves. He is ready to be the judge, the president of
university, corporation, or nation.

63 to 77 (Homo Sapiens)

In the concluding stage of life, man is neither singly Homo
Ludens nor Homo Faber; he is the sage, Utnapishtim, the
survivor of catastrophes, the old man of the mountains to
whom the great and powerful king of Uruk, Gilgamesh, goes
in search of wisdom and freedom from the terror of death.
Here the sage expresses the wisdom and authority of the
human race as opposed to the skill and power of those who
happen to be ruling at the moment. The end of life is a meditation on one's karma, a contemplation on all that has gone
before. This contemplative mode of being is neither work
nor play, and thus those who choose to see old age as the
absence of work, and therefore the presence of play, greatly
mistake it. In the final phase there is a return to the facts of
life in facing the one fact of death. The mind holds on to each
ache or pain; it pays almost a ritual attention to the day's
news and hopes to preserve life by heaping up its facts.

People who think that the end of life is play and a return to Homo Ludens in retirement do not recognize how most people hate retirement and compensatorily hold on to objects and facts for all that they are worth. Old people are supremely the people of opinions, and it is not important whether the opinions are right or wrong, for they are old enough to know how complicated all that is; rather, it is important that opinions are held, for in holding on to them one holds on to life.

Because old age is the contemplative stage of life, it is perhaps best expressed by geniuses who live the life of the mind and spirit. No one takes the paint brushes away from a Picasso and tells him that he must retire. Many geniuses seem to be at their best in old age: one thinks of Yeats, Shaw, Whitehead, Frank Lloyd Wright. Businessmen, however, often die of heart attacks a year or so after they retire. Since they regarded life to be a line on a productivity chart, the end of production spells, for them, the end of life.

An understanding of the cycles of life helps us to see that it contains a dynamic quality that is not met by our linear institutions. In industrial society our institutions do not work for teenagers, women, and old people; they work only for people who are concerned with power and making money. Our institutions demand that people do not make waves, that they stand in line and wait, wait for promotions, raises, and degrees. The image of the production line dominates all our institutions, cultural or economic. But now that the Industrial Revolution has reached its limit to growth, a new cultural revolution is taking place and the priorities of life are being set in the scale against GNPs and Ph.D.s.

This revolution is one in which the energy of culture shifts from institutions to the whole environment. Religion moves out of churches, education moves out of schools, business moves out of factories, and politics moves out of the party system. Through the impact of new informational technology like cable television there is a return to the New England town meeting, and candidates can begin to run for Congress on purely local issues and concerns without having to be *machers* in the Republican or Democratic Party. Naturally, this release of energy from institutions to the entire environment seems like an explosion to people on the inside. Failing to understand these positive releases of human potential, they try to block them.

The most immediate attempt to block the cultural transformation is management's effort to maintain industrial values and procedures through its institutional power in business, government, universities, and foundations. In the Industrial Revolution, culture surrounded nature and made it into a content in its larger structure. In the Great Exhibition of 1851 in London, a controversy over cutting down the trees in Hyde Park was resolved by building the wrought-iron-and-glass structure around them. Now in postindustrial culture management is trying to surround human culture in order to make it into a content in its larger structure, and that is what the education business is really all about.

Once *laissez-faire* provided the ideological apology for industrial development; now the behavioral sciences are trying to provide an apology for the management of a technological society. As government moves away from representational democracy to executive management, so the university moves away from a critical to a consulting role. The power of government and the authority of education are collapsed together into a single ideology called "the sciences of human management." And just as once there was no appeal from the power of the Church without risking damnation, so now there is no appeal from the power of science without risking a charge of irrationality or insanity. Of course, the behavioral sciences are not really scientific, any more than the Established Church in nineteenth-century

England was really holy. Once, it was useful to the ruling class to have the younger sons in the Church, for this lent an air of respectability to its rule and disguised naked power with the more civilized vestments of the Anglican Church. Now we no longer respect these vestments, and so the ruling class has changed them to doctoral robes from Harvard. With its Bundys, Moynihans, and Kissingers, Harvard has become the Canterbury Cathedral of the Established Church of postindustrial society.

This binding of authority and power is a very unhealthy thing for the Republic. In the nineteenth century the scholar had no power, and only the robber-baron capitalism of a Jay Gould could have the ear of a President. In *The Education of Henry Adams,* Adams describes his own attempts to take up residence in Grant's Washington in the hope of securing an appointment. But in a Washington as corrupt as Grant's the services of a Henry Adams were not needed. Luckily, at that time American culture had more dimensions than the political one, and a timely invitation from President Charles Eliot returned Adams to Cambridge and a professorship at Harvard. In the nineteenth century Harvard, the inheritor of the Puritan ethic, was the center of American intellectual and moral authority; Washington was the capital of power, but the distance between Cambridge and Washington expressed the healthy distance between authority and power.

Nineteenth-century Harvard could function as a refuge for the fuller values of a healthy culture, and there the scholar could complain that no one listened to him, but out of his isolation he could create the works that go to make up a civilization. Unfortunately, the scholar was not happy in his isolation; he fancied that if only he had a voice in power, the country would begin to move into a golden age. Now, having lived through a golden age in which "The Best and the

Brightest" sat at the right hand of the father, we can begin to see just how disastrous it is to turn Harvard into a stopover on the way to Washington.

Now big business and big government have been joined by big foundations and big education. Culture has collapsed into society, and society has been compressed into the very narrow range of Republican-Democratic politics. The university, now dependent upon government support, has become the major center of distribution for the new ideology of human management. But with its success has come a deeper failure. Just as once in the nineteenth century the university took authority away from the Church, so now the new culture is beginning to take authority away from the university. To be sure, the university will not disappear, just as the Church did not disappear; but as the Church was to the Berkeleys and Harvards of the fifties and sixties, so will the Berkeleys and Harvards be to the new cultural centers in the seventies and eighties.

To understand the failure of the modern university, one must understand the failure of social science to provide a secular ideology strong enough and culturally deep enough to support the growth of a planetary civilization. All it could do was bring Indian intellectuals to the Center for Advanced Study in the Behavioral Sciences in Palo Alto and teach them how to drink Scotch. Even then, it did not always work, for some of the brighter ones began to realize that American social science, so lavishly supported by the Ford Foundation, was simply ideological camouflage for the spread of a world view congenial to the growth of American-based multinational corporations. The failure of the modern university is thus intimately linked with the failure of social science.

The university was first a village, and then in the days of Oxford and Cambridge it became a town; in the era of Harvard and Berkeley it became a city-state. Now, through the Kissingers and Skinners of Harvard, the tiny city-state, like an ancient Rome, is growing to become the new empire of behavioral civilization. Because history is in the humanities it has no place in "value-free" social science; and so what is missing in the grand imperial vision is an historical memory and a tragic sense that a society which seeks to live like an empire will die like one.

THREE

The Individual as Institution

We all have become so used to certain clichés that even in growing beyond them we still cling to them—as if they were the trellis upon which our contemporary wildness depended. No cliché is more basic to the age than that the individual is powerless in the face of the huge corporations of the post-industrial state. Our society has convinced us that no cultural movement can succeed without political power behind it, and that political power can only be expressed by the heaping up of units in great masses, dollars or votes. Even those opposed to the domination of the huge corporations have accepted these terms of values and have tried to effect a cultural transformation by heaping up great numbers of people in mass demonstrations. From the sociology of the fifties to the New Left radicalism of the sixties, we have held on to the notion that corporation and machine have eliminated the usefulness of individuated man.

If the society of production and protest works in terms of mass and units, nature and culture do not. The anonymous unit rests in the mass, and the mass is indifferent to it, but the unique individual moves in the universal, and the universal is moved by him. No society can stand against the universe for long, but individuals have been standing against society since history began. The individual has not been passed over; it is he who is passing over the institutions of corporation, university, novel, and play to become an institution in himself.

In the deceptiveness of mirror-images, it seemed for a while as if rugged individualist had been replaced by competent management team, as if artist had been replaced by film company and theatrical troupe. But the artist who was sensitive to this cultural shift from the personal *object* of art to the communal *process* of artistic happenings could no longer be content with merely writing novels; he had to use the old form of the novel as a means of creating the new form of the individual as institution. With a new anarchic planetary culture stretching the shape of the old industrial nation-states, the novelist, like Norman Mailer or Ken Kesey, could not contain himself. If technology sent man out in metal manufactured by conglomerate NASA, the new culture sent man out of his old containers by and through his self.

Paolo Soleri, Ivan Illich, Ralph Nader, Andy Warhol, Buckminster Fuller, Alan Watts, Timothy Leary, John Lilly, and Edgar Mitchell: all were men who left institutions behind to become institutions in their own right. Paradoxically enough, it was the colossal scale of media society that enabled them to become independent.

The rise of the individual as institution, of course, stimulates a change in the old corporate institutions. The rise of Ralph Nader, the public individual, and the stumbling of Lockheed, the private corporation, are culturally interrelated phenomena: both express the social transformation of the Second Industrial Revolution generated in the United States by World War II.

Ironically, it was the technology America used to protect its private enterprise system that signaled the end of that system. Our victory contained defeat—just as the defeats of

Germany and Japan contained hidden victories. As private university and private corporation became public-service corporate systems supported by government funds, the meaning of private space dissolved in the "public sector." The institutional ceremonial robes of officer, clergyman, professor, and businessman no longer held attraction; careers lost their private meaning in a world of temporary and interchangeable roles in corporate systems. Since the corporation could not reverse this trend without abandoning its success, it contributed to its own demise and the old ideology of business began to fail as an explanation of what state capitalism was all about.

Given the problems of pollution and the principle that all things must grow or stagnate, it becomes clear that because General Motors cannot grow, but, at best, can only hope to hold its own in social circumstances highly unfavorable to the automobile, its future looks much dimmer than Ralph Nader's.

One need neither grieve nor rejoice. We are witnessing not so much the destruction of corporations as the de-structuring of society. Just as the novelist walked out of print into life, so the corporation can walk out of business into life. The old seventeenth-century stockholding corporation can become a communal ark in a sea of public-service corporate systems. New Yorkers can form private corporations in which culturally similar groups of people, be they WASPs, hippies, blacks, swingers, or Sufis, can own their own apartment buildings, security forces, communal schools, cable TV channels, in-house magazines, and New England farm retreats.

As people walk out of the old containers, the energy released will stimulate the growth of a whole new kind of political economy. If we pay farmers not to grow corn, then we can pay eighteen-year-olds not to go to college. We can think along the lines of Ivan Illich and save the money we are wasting on elaborate campus-containers by giving each eighteen-year-old an outright grant of $3,000. The individual could blow it on a trip to Europe; or he could join with friends in buying a farm, putting out a record album, book, or magazine, or opening up a handcrafts boutique. If, instead of spending the money, he chose to let it accumulate interest in his citizen's account, then by the time he was at the right age for university, his funds could finance his entire education. In such a socialized system of anarchic capitalism, each individual could institutionalize himself in his own imaginative way. In terms of education, we could say that in such a culture the campus is nowhere and the university is everywhere.

Even without government grants to eighteen-year-olds, romantic, artistic capitalism has now become a radical instrument for effecting cultural change. To work for cultural change *within* SUNY, SDS, or HEW is to be facing in the wrong historical direction. Universities, radical organizations, and governmental agencies are filled with experts, and experts are right only about what has been and not about what can be. Expert mathematicians proved with an elegant formula that no machine could ever fly, but two bicycle repairmen went into the air anyway. If we supported our eighteen-year-olds with the trust of direct grants rather than forced internment in youth reservations, we might find other inventive amateurs embarrassing the experts.

The creative individual leaves the universities and the government agencies behind to move out into a new space, but the political radical stays behind. Like a guilt-ridden Samson he is attracted to the Philistines and can only mask his guilt by bringing the whole thing down on top of himself. The imaginative individual must walk out because he wishes to create new things rather than destroy old ones. The man who shoots horses as a way of changing agrarian society does not invent automobiles; the man who bombs refineries as a way of changing automotive society does not design cities in which cars are unnecessary.

One such imaginative individual as institution is Paolo Soleri in his Cosanti Foundation in Arizona. Cosanti, or *anti cosa*, means "anti-thing,"and in his work against the things of a materialistic society, Soleri is moving, without the help of government agencies, foundations, universities, architectural firms, or developers, toward redesigning the urban civilization of earth. To support himself in this work, he makes and sells wind-bells cast from bronze; he writes, lectures, and charges tuition ($270) to students who come to work as laborer-apprentices for a month. Seventy miles outside Phoenix, Soleri and his apprentices are attempting to start the urban revolution of Sumer all over again. Arcosanti is the name of this, the world's first "arcology," and in its wealth of imagination and dearth of funds it is all a capitalism of a fundamentalist purity that would shame the revisionist tendencies of a Boeing or a North American Rockwell. In its combination of primitiveness and daring, Arcosanti is like the Watts Towers of another independent Italian-American builder, Simon Rodia. Perhaps if each student had his $3,000 grant from the government, more students could afford to stay longer, and Soleri could complete Arcosanti to prove whether it is architecture or the art of assemblage.

There is no doubt in Soleri's mind, and that is why he has had the guts to risk everything to build his Noah's ark amid the laughter of decadent urbanites. "Arcology" is what Soleri calls his union of architecture and ecology, but it is even more than that, for this student of Teilhard de Chardin has made arcology a consummation of the evolutionary process itself. When you spread Soleri's four-foot-wide testament, *Arcology: The City in the Image of Man*,[1] before you, there is no comfortable way of looking at it except on your knees. If you were to place the folio on your desk, you would have to clear everything of your own out of its way. And yet for all the folio's pomp and circumstance, you do not feel threatened or overwhelmed, but fascinated: like a kid on the floor with the Sunday comics. The book has a science fiction enormity of vision that is totally missing in the countless academic monographs produced by professors of this-and-that. In fact, some of the drawings do recall the fantasy cities of the science fiction comic books of the forties. Here the city is seen not in terms of groovy little ethnic neighborhoods for radical chic, computer models for liberals, or tax bases for conservatives, but as the cultural vehicle in which man has made and is still making his evolutionary journey.

Evolution moves against the direction of entropy; as matter moves toward more probable states of maximum molecular disorder, life moves toward increasingly more improbable states of maximum molecular organization. More and more is packed into less and less, until the miniaturization process reaches its greatest level of what Teilhard calls "complexification" in the compactness of the human brain. The simplicity of its size and shape belies the dazzling complexity of its interior. For Soleri this process of complexification linked with miniaturization is the lesson the city planner should take away from the study of nature. In evolution, simplicity is always linked to complexity: while huge dinosaurs lumber into extinction, tiny mammals chatter in the trees. Soleri would say it is much the same with our cities now. The huge megalopolitan beasts are sprawling all over the earth; in terms of thermodynamics, they are spreading their energy equitably through space and approaching the heat-death of entropy. They destroy the earth, turn farmland into parking lots, and waste enormous amounts of time and energy transporting people, goods, and services over their expanses. They so fill their ecological niche that they destroy it, and thus become caught in their own evolutionary dead end.

Soleri's answer is urban implosion rather than explosion.

The city should contract and intensify, but in order to hold its information in negentropic form, it should imitate evolution and complexify itself through intense miniaturization. A city of 600,000 should become a single, recycling, organic arcology. The people would live not crowded in ghettos but on the outer skin of a towering arcology that faced toward a nature that was once again natural. Thus the surface of an arcology would be "a membrane and not a wall." Inside the arcology, along its central spinal axis, would be not the natural but the civic space. Here society would turn inward for the concerns of man and culture. In some of the drawings of the arcologies, Soleri has marked off areas as "commercial," "cultural," and "civic," as if these historically rooted distinctions would still exist in a truly futuristic civilization. When I asked Soleri if he didn't think it contradictory to be so far-out in one direction but so conventional in another, I realized in just looking at him that my answer was already expressed in his appearance. A short and very thin middle-aged man, Soleri was a taut figure of hard line and flat plane; with his gray hair brushed over his forehead, his aristocratic features gave him the air of a classical Roman senator, an air which was nicely contradicted by the red-and-blue-striped tank top *cum* brass-buttoned hot pants that he was wearing. He leaned back with his legs crossed and his hands cupping his knees, and as he thought, his body toughened and took up the slack like a suspension bridge reacting to the weight crossing it; and then he answered me: "There are conventional distinctions that will still exist in the future city; we will not excrete in the postal system or flush letters down the toilet."

For all his apparent visionary perspective, Soleri has a craftsman's sense of detail and practicality. He envisions no ESP communications system or matter-disintegrating toilets; and although it looks as if it would take a power system based on thermonuclear fusion to drive an arcology, he insists that an arcology would be simpler to operate than New

York—a point most New Yorkers would readily concede. Because his arcologies do have such a comic-book science fiction appearance, Soleri is quite insistent on their practical feasibility in the present.

Soleri's practicality becomes much clearer when one realizes that he is not a futurist at all, but a conservative. The anthropologist A. F. C. Wallace has given us a model of the prophet of a nativistic movement, and his model helps in recognizing Soleri's cultural implications.[2] Wallace says that when a culture is in a period of extreme stress brought on by maximum cultural distortion, prophets arise to reformulate the traditional path through the mazeway of nature, self, and society. In our case it is not the Ghost Dance of the Plains Indians, but the ghost dance of Western, industrial, urban civilization. The greatest cities of the world—London, Paris, Rome, New York, and Tokyo—are becoming the most uncivilized places of all, and for every year they survive, another decade is taken off the prognosis for the earth's atmosphere. Something has to be done. Moses left Egypt and went to the desert, not to stay there forever but to find the transforming space in which to change himself and return to history to create a new nation. Soleri is in the desert, not to escape the city for some pastoral dream but to create a wholly new urban civilization. He is a nativistic prophet who wishes to uphold the old in ways radical enough to ensure its survival in the future.

Soleri believes that it is the city with its institutions that humanizes man, and so he rejects hippie communes as places where men try to relate to one another in human ways by stripping themselves of the very things that make them human.

Who but the mad and the dead would be willing to give up as of this moment the access (for man) to the written universe, to the music of man, to the world of his mind which he has physically constructed, to the institution itself of civilization on the presumption that after all what counts is the direct relationship between what at such a degree of deprivation would not be more than two or more naked apes?[3]

When Carlos Castaneda goes into the desert, he tries to move away from the heritage of his Italian father to discover the older heritage of the grandfather of the race, the shaman, Don Juan. For Castaneda isolation in the desert is a psychedelic technique for projecting the unconscious, but for Soleri the desert is the Archimedean place to stand to move the cities of the earth. Soleri does not indulge in youth-culture fantasies about mysticism and nature; for him human nature is the only nature possible to us.

The giant is absurdly tearing itself apart, escaping into the non-self, the naught of mental abstraction called nature, that barrel of illusions, melancholy and dark pessimism, that portrait by a mad painter, by a week-end poet at a loss for "things to do," that fantasy of the "outdoorsman," that mind-fabricated enchantress. Nature is far more and far beyond such fabrications. It is the furnace of the sun.[4]

From Soleri's Aristotelian point of view, biological man is the polis-dwelling animal. Beethoven on a desert island would not whistle in sonata form. The attempt to run off to a desert island is thus an attempt to escape the tension of forms in which creation is possible. The acidhead on the commune is still a child of the suburbs: he is a mutation of the parental virus that infected the cities; but from nature's point of view his chemically polluted brain is still a foreign body. The hippie commune is, therefore, the farthest perimeter of the explosion of megalopolis. For Soleri, the way out is not far-out, but far-in: implosion, not explosion.

The city must contract, intensify, and miniaturize civilization. But for Western man a life as a cell on the skin of an arcology would seem evolutionary all right: the evolution that took the independent and self-sufficient amoeba and turned it into specialized bone, nerve, and muscle tissue and told it to stay in its place in the new higher organism. Simply because Soleri's arcologies do look like organisms, they give many people the creeps and have them shuddering with exclamations of "anthill." In their instinctive response is the recognition that evolution means business and there is no sense talking about it unless you are willing to experience the complete transformation of human life, mental as well as architectural. In their reflex action they touch Soleri's blind spot.

If a man is to find his place in an arcology, he must not move about in bourgeois upward mobility; he must not move about in the ecologically burdensome culture of wealth with its cars, Ski-Doos, and cabin crusiers. Like a man in the Middle Ages he must know his place, and like a man in the Middle Ages to know his place he must live in a spiritual culture that makes up for all the toys he has lost from the old bourgeois, materialistic, and democratic days.

The return of the Middle Ages is clear in Soleri's thought. Apostate or not, Soleri's culture is Catholic, and his arcologies are medieval cathedral towns.

> Is there any difference between the aim of the city and the aim of the Catholic (universal) Church? They are one and the same. In a very physical way, the city is the Church.[5]

Soleri's Catholic background is no incidental issue. If the Club of Rome's "Project on the Predicament of Mankind" is correct and we have reached "The Limits to Growth,"[6] then we have also reached the limits of "The Protestant Ethic and the Spirit of Capitalism" that spurred that growth. The period from the sixteenth century to the present has been a Protestant period, one of humanism, democracy, mechanization, and the secularization of the arts. It was a period of creative expansion, energy, disequilibrium, and dissonance. If we are sensing that we have had too much growth without order, it is natural that a compensatory movement would look to the concentric, hierarchical, sacred, nonmechanistic values of the Catholic world view. Such a movement would be one of consolidation rather than expansion.

But we should not kid ourselves about what is involved in such a movement. The *Roman* Catholic Church, as any good Conservative Christian Anarchist knows, is not the Mystical Body of Christ. In the Mystical Body of Christ, at the very end of human spiritual evolution, the *more* one expresses his uniqueness and his absolute freedom, the more truly he relates to the ecstatic whole of the single being that is mankind. Any attempt to realize this transcendental state in institutional terms leads to very nontranscendental forms of political collectivization. The Roman Church tried to hold power under the aspect of eternity, and as a result it became an imperial, authoritarian, collectivizing, and totalitarian institution. Out of this institutionalization of the ineffable came the kind of thought that saw man becoming religious through, and only through, the collectivization of the Church. At its best, this kind of thought produced the Cathedral of Chartres and the music of Guillaume de Machaut; at its worst, it produced the Inquisitor who could torture a man's body while firmly believing that he was compassionately doing his best to save the man's soul from heresy: for after all, the torture of the body lasts only a few hours or days, but the torture of the soul in hell lasts for eternity. In following Teilhard de Chardin, Soleri has inherited all the political ambiguities of that Catholic thinker.

Although our individualistic instincts may rebel against this drive toward the collective, they do so in vain and wrongly. In vain, because no power in the world can enable us to escape from what is in itself the power of the world. And wrongly because the real nature of this impulse that is sweeping us toward a state of super-organization is such as to make us more completely personalized and human. . . .

The very fact of becoming aware of this profound ordering of things may enable human collectivization to pass beyond the enforced phase, where it is now, into the free phase.[7]

How the mysticism of Teilhard can be carried over into city planning can be seen in Soleri's views on the relationship between the biological organism and the arcological organism, "the organism of a thousand minds":

If we ever have a superorganism made up of men, men retaining their own uniqueness, then such an organism will be made up of thousands or millions or more of brains. Furthermore, each of those brains will contain a mind, that is to say, will overgovern that power of choice among the endless propositions of the possible, the one-at-a-time performances making the present.

This will be the fundamental distinction between the city and the anthill, the beehive, the termite colony, and so on: not just brains by the score but also minds by the score. The romantic and rugged individualists will speak out immediately about the mindlessness of the human beehive. They might want to glance at nightmarish suburbia with its six billion individuals; but it is their privilege not to reason about mankind and the staggering logistics it is faced with.[8]

Soleri, the individual as institution, paradoxically becomes the spokesman for the collectivization of mankind. The contemporary phenomenon of the individual as institution could thus be the beginning of an *enantidromia*, a dialectical movement that begins in one position but ends up in the directly opposite position: for example, the rise of the *masses* in industrial society was a movement toward the *individual* free of the aristocracy, the Church, and the extended family. Soleri, the individual, could become, like the eye of the needle, a tiny space through which the whole of mankind is sewn together.

It is significant that Soleri singles out suburbia for his condemnation, for the suburban city is quintessentially an expression of Protestant mass culture. Robert Fogelson, in his history of Los Angeles,[9] has pointed out that nineteenth- and early-twentieth-century Los Angeles was settled by white, Protestant Midwesterners who brought to the city a yeoman's suspicion of the Eastern city with its tenements teeming with Semites and Irishmen. Boston and New York represented everything they loathed: community was seen as crowding, neighborhoods were seen as ghettos. They approached city planning with the grid of rural surveying and laid out the ideal as a pastoral city in which each yeoman stood upon his plot of ground. Over the years, of course, this ideal became the house with swimming pool and two-car garage, but no room for grandparents, the isolated warehouse of appliances from which the children were shipped in station wagons from one prearranged experience to another. And when later the children produced in these warehouses turned out to be hippies in search of spontaneous experience and communal living, their parents blamed them for not having learned about life through the school of hard knocks, the Depression, the war—all the experience from which they had been protected.

Rugged individualism, private enterprise, independence from tradition and the extended family: these are the deeply held values of American Protestantism, and since American Protestantism is our dominant culture, these become the values of all Jews, Irishmen, Mexicans, and Puerto Ricans who make it. But many an Irishman or Jew who leaves the old neighborhood to move out to the suburbs finds that it is not all that he hoped for, but that, in fact, his new freedom has brought with it a new sense of alienation. Out of the experience of this alienation, the spilled-over suburban city begins to clot and congeal into the pseudo neighborhoods of swinging singles, PTA hamlets, divorce condominiums, and geriatric ghettos. But the secular, deracinated, and desperately hedonistic culture of these clots is far too thin to stop the city from hemorrhaging.

Thus it is not surprising that the Catholic critics of contemporary culture see the need for a movement from secular disintegration to sacral reintegration. In this sense, the ideas of Soleri should be compared with those of another Catholic critic of contemporary culture, Marshall McLuhan:

> I'm saying that the result, not the current process, of retribalization makes us reactionary in our basic attitudes and values. Once we are enmeshed in the magical resonance of the tribal echo chamber, the debunking of myths and legends is replaced by their religious study. Within the consensual framework of tribal values, there will be few if any rebels who challenge the tribe itself. . . .
>
> Psychic communal integration, made possible at last by the electronic media, could create the universality of consciousness foreseen by Dante when he predicted that men would continue as no more than broken fragments until they were unified into an inclusive consciousness. In a Christian sense, this is merely a new interpretation of the mystical body of Christ; and Christ, after all, is the ultimate extension of man.[10]

When McLuhan looks into the future, he looks into his own rear-view mirror and sees the future as the Middle Ages, for the medieval *image* has always appealed to intellectuals recoiling from the savagery of industrialization. After the first wave of the Industrial Revolution from 1770 to 1851, England itself seemed to be in a mood for consolidation; and in "The Medieval Court" designed by Pugin for the Crystal Palace of the Great Exhibition of 1851, it took a nostalgic look at the European civilization it had helped to destroy. With Pugin, William Morris, Matthew Arnold, and Cardinal Newman, medievalism became one of the first countercultures to industrialism.

Now that the first wave of the American postwar Second Industrial Revolution is over, it is not surprising that people are in a mood for an internal restructuring of human culture. With the age of the rugged entrepreneur over, the new post-industrial manager has the sense of institutional corporate politics of a Catholic cardinal. Aurelio Peccei with his Club of Rome is a clear example of a multinational manager in search of a new concentric order. In his book *The Chasm Ahead*,[11] Peccei longs for a new kind of ecclesiastical hierarchy and wishes to see "The Great Four" (America, Europe, Russia, and Japan) create a planetary interlocking directorate to overcome our ecological crisis and establish a new reverence for civilization and Holy Mother Nature. Because these new managers have such Vatican sensibilities, it is small wonder that some students of multinational corporations see them as reminders of another era.

The position of the companies is, in some ways, analogous to that of the Catholic Church in the past. Kings and emperors frequently felt their positions to be overshadowed by its international organization, its influence on national policies, and its immense buildings and tracts of land.[12]

While Peccei is working for a transformation at the top, another Catholic critic of contemporary society, Ivan Illich, is working on the very foundation of bourgeois, Protestant society—the school. By attempting to "deschool society,"[13] Illich is challenging the basic secular institution responsible for bourgeois upward mobility. In a manner that is more anarchist Catholic than Roman, he is trying to separate the authority of the mind from the power of the educational system. Illich's neofeudal world view is a vision of elites bound together in a culture of voluntary poverty. Only in this way can a civilization be recreated in which wealth has no charisma and the billions of poor have a chance to aspire to a condition of human dignity that has nothing to do with achieving an American standard of living. By eliminating the vicious cycle of the revolution of rising expectations in the Third World, Illich would hope to find ways in which mankind can adjust to the facts of life in a world set by "The Limits to Growth." From a Marxist point of view, of course, this is counterrevolutionary propaganda; better that the revolution of rising expectations create a hundred Cubas (though it is more likely to create a hundred Brazils). But Marxists are nothing if not industrial-age materialists, and so we must assume that they are falling back into the wake of history along with their linked opposites, the Protestant, bourgeois industrial capitalists.

It is precisely this separation of authority from power that unites the Catholic sensibilities of Ivan Illich and Paolo Soleri. At a conference on "Thinking on a Planetary Scale," held at York University in Toronto, Soleri presented a slide lecture on the arcological approach to urban civilization. As always happens, some people recoiled in shivers of claustrophobic horror and spoke of beehives. One student accused Soleri of being a fascist because at his Cosanti Foundation the students had to work as the master directed them; there was no participatory democracy in the design of Arcosanti. Soleri responded: "You don't understand. I have no *power* over my students. They are free to come and go. I have only *authority*. If they come to me because of my authority, and then do not respect that authority, they have no reason for coming to study and work with me. Authority has the power of conviction. Authoritarianism has the power of coercion." But the student missed Soleri's point. He was ignorant of the tradition of the Renaissance artist in his atelier, and the word "fascist" seemed to exhaust his whole historical vocabulary. So caught up was he in the cant of "free" schools that he could not see that that kind of education contains more subtle forms of manipulation and "behavioral modification" than Soleri's mastership.

The separation of authority from power is not easily understood in terms of American culture. We based a whole revolution on rejecting European authority and power and lumped geniuses, lords, and cardinals all together into one untrustworthy group. It is, therefore, an historical irony that the country that rejected kings and crowns ended up by idolizing the Presidency and allowed the holder of the office to become more powerful than any Caesar. Lacking the European traditions of culture, Americans collapsed culture into society and made greatness identical with the political leadership of that society. Every boy should want to grow up to be President, and every President should be an Abraham Lincoln, for the only place for a man to be great in America is in the *White* House. Fortunately, Watergate has broken the spell and now Americans have a chance to create a Republic worth celebrating in 1976. In the meantime we are still holding on to the notion that wealth and power are what civilization is all about. When Einstein used his uncashed paycheck from Princeton as a bookmark, the incident became a legend—not of wisdom, but of how stupid the most intelligent man in the world could be. The legend confirmed the average American in his conviction that the wise guys weren't smart enough to come in out of the rain. And when Ralph Nader refused to use his victory over General Motors as a start for a campaign for political office, many felt that he was missing his chance.

In hoping to create or maintain a civilization in the wake of the devastation of industrialization, conservatives like Nader are eager to affirm the values of truth, honesty, and community. Nader's life of voluntary poverty would confirm Ivan Illich's prediction about the neo-Benedictine way of life of the new elites. By giving up wealth and power, the cultural leader is emphasizing that a culture is more than a social structure. Gandhi never became President of India. When Americans want Nader to run for President, they show how difficult it is for them to conceive of any human culture separate from the politics of wealth and power. Europe had a civilization before the Industrial Revolution; America did not, so it is small wonder that the limits to our cultural imagination are set by industrial institutions like the university. It is also small wonder that it takes Europeans like Paolo Soleri or Ivan Illich to remind us that in healthy cultures prophet and king are not one and the same man.

The separation of authority from power is the most important feature of the individual as institution, for in working without the powerful resources and rewards of existing institutions, the individual is trying to create new cultural sources of authority. If Nader were a Senator, if Illich were a dean of a School of Education, if Soleri were a director of an architectural firm, each would lose his most critical freedom in achieving the power to act. When the Old Testament Hebrew prophet moved out of his primitive surroundings into the palace of King David, he became, not a Samuel, but a Nathan, the Henry Kissinger of his time.

In the collision of values between good and evil, authority and power, freedom and necessity, there is a scattering of values in which morality cannot be isolated into any one political position. But perhaps the diagram on the next page will make this clearer.

What this mandala enables us to see is the structural identity between mirror opposites. There is an identity between the power of the ruling conservatives and liberals and the terror of the extreme radicals and reactionaries: one sector has power, one wishes to get it. In each case the world view is based not on civilization but on force. At right angles to the opposition between these two groups is a quite different association. On the right side of the mandala in the white sector are the conservatives and reactionaries who believe in the values of *traditional* civilization; they are the forces of order as opposed to energy, the followers of Burke rather

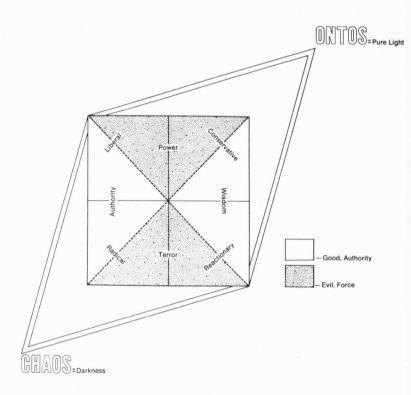

than Blake. On the left side in the white sector are the liberals and radicals who wish to raise civilization to new ideals not contained in the tradition. In the white sector are found the men of good will, the men of full human culture; in the dotted sector are found the men of ill will, the men whose only culture is power. What the mandala enables us to see is that a civilization is a culture larger than any political party, Left or Right, and that in this larger culture men of values are found in all the four basic political orientations—conservative, reactionary, radical, and liberal. Though ideologues may try to lock all human values into one party, revolutionary or established, human culture is a complex field in which a value is defined and achieved in conflict with its opposite. Truth is not found *in* either conservative or revolutionary; truth is the magnetic field that surrounds those two poles.

Once we see the basic point of the mandala, we can see why it is necessary to respect the difference between authority and power. In the American Constitution we have tried to lodge authority in the Supreme Court and power in Congress and the Executive, but the Supreme Court is still the judicial branch of the government, and as such it is, as the Warren Court proved, a very powerful branch of that government. For a time in European civilization the Church was the institution of wisdom and authority. But in the year 1600 the modern scientific age began, as Whitehead has pointed out, with the sacrifice at the stake of its first martyr, Giordano Bruno. When the Church robed itself in Inquisitional power, it robbed itself of its spiritual authority. For a time in American civilization the university was the institution of wisdom and authority, but when in World War II the government led the university into research in weapons and behavioral-science controls, it destroyed the university's authority by giving it power. But because all things are bound together in chains of action and reaction, the very postwar technology that created the multiversity also created the new informational culture in which the individual could walk out of the ivy corridors of power. Now there are new voices speaking to the students; and whether it is Richard Alpert at the Lama Foundation in New Mexico, Ivan Illich in CIDOC in Mexico, or Paolo Soleri at the Cosanti Foundation in Arizona, the students are listening to and respecting forms of authority they would not tolerate at Harvard or Berkeley.

The vision of Catholics like Soleri and Illich is medieval, but it is really closer to the primitive austerity of the Dark Ages than to the cultural fluorescence of the High Middle Ages. By moving to the edges of our urban civilization in Arizona and Mexico, these men are following the tradition of the monks in the monastery schools of the Dark Ages. Soleri is quite consciously working in this monastic tradition:

In the West it was the monastery that faced the megamachine of the secular establishment (military and paramilitary) then in a state of disrepair; insisting on the nonautomatism of man, it upheld the cultural level of society. Now that automatism of the mental is menacingly appearing as a pale reflection of the burgeoning monster flower of automation, nothing would serve man better than a restoration, on necessarily new levels, of the psychological and mental primacy of the species. The new monastery must be the secular city, or at least its core, the learning center.[14]

If we are facing a possible return to the Dark Ages, as many scientists and scholars fear, then it is natural that Western men think back upon the tradition of the monastery school as a way of preserving civilization. But Soleri is naïve if he thinks that we can have the spirit of the tough and austere monastic centers in a secular city or experimental college. In the years since World War II we have built new universities and experimental colleges by the score, and still the cultural disintegration goes on. In fact, in many cases, civilization now has to be protected from the universities. The spirit of the monasteries of Iona and Lindisfarne cannot be so easily packaged into an arcology.

If we are to have another Lindisfarne, it must be more than Soleri's secular city or learning center; it must be a transformer in which the energy of man's cultural evolution is stepped up to another level. In fact, just such a place already exists in Auroville, the planetary city now being built by the Sri Aurobindo Ashram near Pondicherry, India. Soleri speaks of "matter becoming spirit," but his approach to this Teilhard vision is artistic. Matter when it is turned into sculpture or architecture is matter becoming spirit. This is what is meant in Soleri's idea of "estheto-genesis." But in the Integral Yoga of Sri Aurobindo much more is involved in the process of transformation. Consciousness is like an FM radio band: as long as one is locked into one station, all he receives is the information of one reality; but if, through the transformation of the sexual energy that holds him into the physical plane of Eros and Thanatos, he is able to move his consciousness to a different station on the FM band, then he discovers universes beyond matter in the cosmic reaches of spirit. In Yoga, the spinal column is the FM band and the chakras along the spine represent the various stations of cosmic information. After one has gone through these universes, he returns to the body, but now the body has been altered by the process and a new nervous system develops in preparation for the continued evolution of man. This is the Resurrection of the Body. As the Christian poet T. S. Eliot described it at the end of *Four Quartets*:

> We shall not cease from exploration
> And the end of all our exploring
> Will be to arrive where we started
> And know the place for the first time. . . .
> When the tongues of flame are in-folded
> Into the crowned knot of fire
> And the fire and the rose are one.

In India the union of the fire and the rose would be called the union of kundalini and the thousand-petaled lotus; in ancient Mexico it would be called teaching the serpent how to fly, how to become a plumed serpent, a quetzalcoatl. The imagery is artistic, but the purpose of the art is to direct one to a spiritual experience. If one stops to admire the expression in verse or stone and does not go on to the experience himself, then he has definitely stopped. Yoga changes the body and the relationship between consciousness and matter, not simply by decorating matter with art, but by altering the very structure of matter and physical space-time. What is merely literary in Soleri is quite literal in Aurobindo.

What the followers of Aurobindo see themselves as doing in Auroville is preparing a new planetary city for a new kind of man. If Arcosanti is a cultural vehicle for urbanly exhausted, entropic man, Auroville is a chrysalis for an entirely new species. As Aurobindo has said: "Man is a transitional being."[15] Art is important at Auroville, but the Aurovillians believe that you cannot solve the problems of human culture with more art, or more architecture; the transformation is cultural, not artistic. Soleri is a Michelangelo, the expressor of a culture rather than the creator of one. But first things must come first. First comes the re-visioning of the universe in Christianity, then comes the Sistine Chapel and the B Minor Mass. One does not live in the Sistine Chapel or the B Minor Mass, one lives in Christianity; and when artists with their strong egos create monuments to themselves for other people to live in, they often find their clients moving out after the novelty has worn off: this happened on several occasions with the residences designed by Soleri's teacher, Frank Lloyd Wright.

Even at Auroville one can feel this difference between residence and monument. The permanent buildings are attractive pieces of sculpture; with their curves and open spaces, they are like oversize works of Henry Moore. It is pleasant and enjoyable to go to school in a sculpture, but one is most at home in Auroville in the temporary thatched huts of the workers. In a brilliant stroke of genius that uses the best of the past in a modern way, the traditional thatched hut has been turned into a more complex polyhedron. With concrete floors replacing the old dirt ones, with triangular panels opening and closing over the old windows, with triangular divisions replacing the old simple rectangular room, the modern thatched hut of Auroville has all the elegance of true simplicity. With a cot to the side of a low wall, a few pillows thrown over it, a straw mat, a bottle with some flowers, how little it takes to live like a king. The huts cluster organically like leaves on a tree; they are not compressed like cells in the trunk. Though I admire the sculptural edifices of Auroville's Roger Anger or Cosanti's Soleri, I would rather live in the huts. But this is merely a matter of personal taste. I prefer Lindisfarne to St. Peter's Basilica, the Chaconne to the St. Matthew Passion, but human culture is greater than individual taste and so has room for both Auroville and Arcosanti.

If Soleri were to accomplish all that he wishes, he would have to be Frank Lloyd Wright, Gandhi, and Aurobindo in one man. Soleri is a very impressive human being; he has both genius and guts, but he is an abbot and not a messiah. Soleri, the Abbot of Cosanti, and Illich, the Abbot of CIDOC, have indeed taken us back in the direction of Lindisfarne, but they have not gone far enough. If one moves Western, secular, aggressive, civilized man into an arcology, the settlement will be no more successful than a public housing development or a British New Town. The arcology, rather than solving the problem of urban civilization, could very well become the ultimate instrument of human collectivization.

When I asked Soleri what was to stop the International Nickel Company from taking an arcology, turning it into a company town like Sudbury, Ontario, ionizing the atmosphere, and making everyone happy and productive, he simply answered: "The compassion of man." But this reply answers nothing, for the compassion of man did not prevent Sudbury or Buchenwald; it was only able to shift the atomic bomb from Kyoto to Hiroshima.

Soleri has given far too little thought to the cultural implications of arcological living. He is so profoundly conservative and European in all matters of contemporary American culture that he cannot recognize that some sections of the young are working on the very ways of living that could make the close fit of life in an arcology no more confining or unnatural than the close fit of the foot in the shoe. In what Jacob Needleman calls "The New Religions"[16] of the young, the emphasis on personal transformation over institutional information is the missing cultural content to Soleri's physical structures. If one has cosmic consciousness, he can go out of the universe into an arcology in the same way that a New Yorker goes out of the city into his apartment. And just as the civilized culture of the New Yorker enables him to put up with the confinements of apartment, subway, and cab, so the culture of the new religions will enable postcivilized man to move in and out of space in a wholly new way.

Soleri is a civilized artist and not a postcivilized mystic and believes that "The most verisimilar concept of God is not analogous to the economist, or the politician, or the lawyer, or the legislator, or the technician, or the priest, but the artist, and it could not be otherwise as it is the artist who is end-oriented while the others are means-oriented."[17] So very much like a Catholic, he regards the mysticism of the young as "quietism." But if each man in an arcology were to be an aesthetic Soleri, a Renaissance Italian artist, he would have to move out to find the space in which to create the physical structures of his own visions. Soleri is something of a paradox; like Frazier in *Walden Two*, he is a man who builds a culture that could never produce him, and a culture he himself could not live in as anything other than its creator. Of course, these contradictions are not unique to Soleri. McLuhan, the avatar of American electronic kitsch, is a nineteenth-century, high-culture Canadian. Ivan Illich, the iconoclast in education, is a Tolstoyan aristocrat in search of his long-lost peasants. Norman O. Brown, the prophet of sexual transfiguration, is an extremely cerebral and very shy classicist. And yet for all his contradictions, Soleri is still one of the most interesting and intelligent speculators in contemporary culture.

Ultimately, perhaps, Soleri's ideas are more exciting than

his designs; like Paxton, whose ideas in wrought iron and glass for the Crystal Palace looked forward to the Bauhaus, Soleri may be pointing in a direction he himself will not reach. Too many of the arcologies look like cultural containers rather than cultural vehicles; and yet when Soleri designs a bridge, the superb craftsman in him takes over and the sinuous beauty of design reappears. Even the ugly names of the arcologies, like Babelnoah, Arckibutz, and Theodiga, disappear, and are replaced with the more graceful English of "Stonebow." In more ways than one, this form expresses Soleri at his best—a builder of bridges over the most difficult cultural abyss man has ever tried to span.

FOUR

The World State and the Shadow of H. G. Wells

A specter is haunting the world, the specter of H. G. Wells. A man of fierce passions in life, in death he remains passionately attached to the earth and cannot let go. On nights when the news is particularly bad you can feel the hold he still has on us. Not until all his visions have been realized and a world state rises upon the ashes of the old nations will his ghost be able to move on. He was never a patient man, but perhaps now that his blood is gone he can stand the waiting. After all, history came so close before.

It was in 1913 that Wells wrote a novel, *The World Set Free*, in which atomic energy was used to make bombs for a war that devastated the world. So horrified was mankind at what it had done that it finally allowed its best men to come forward and build a better world. Nuclear war and world states run by scientists were wild ideas in 1913, but by the autumn of 1936 the holiday guests at Niels Bohr's house, Lord Rutherford and Werner Heisenberg, stopped a moment to give the idea a fleeting thought. It was Heisenberg who remarked: "I believe there is an English science fiction story in which a physicist solves his country's difficulties, at home and abroad, by producing an atom bomb as a kind of *deus ex machina*. All that is, of course, nothing but wishful thinking."[1] But Leo Szilard had read the book and so could not so quickly pass over it. When the idea for setting up a chain reaction occurred to him, Szilard thought again of Wells:

> Knowing what this would mean—and I knew it because I had read Wells—I did not want this patent to become public. The only way to keep it from becoming public was to assign it to the Government. So I assigned the patent to the British Admiralty.[2]

It took the physical scientists about thirty years to catch up with Wells. Naturally, it is taking the social scientists much longer, but it is beginning to be clear that scholarship is taking on the ideas of science fiction.[3] Around the world a group of scholars, each one prominent in his own nation, is gathering to produce a vision of a desirable world for the nineties. This "World Order Models Project" is the work of the Institute for World Order, and its monographs will be published in the near future. However, one of its "World Order Books" has already appeared, and, appropriately enough, the book is the work of the historian and H. G. Wells scholar, W. Warren Wagar.[4]

When one considers the World Order Models Project along with the better-known Club of Rome's "Project on the Predicament of Mankind,"[5] he can see that of Wells's two basic strategies for achieving the world state, the "Open Conspiracy" and the secret "freemasonry of science," the first has already been put into action by these two associations. Professor Wagar, however, is still more taken with the secret, conspiratorial approach to world government. Since his approach is explicitly about world takeover, whereas the Club of Rome's approach is limited to world management, it is perhaps better to begin with the futurist fantasies of Wagar and end with the immediate actions of the Club of Rome.

It is an interesting paradox that when a scholar tries to take the ideas of science fiction literally and propound them without fictional artifice there is often such a loss of strength and vision that it is hard to take the monograph seriously. It is almost as if the scholar had tried to write his doctoral dissertation out of a dream or a love affair. Since there is very little in Wagar that is not better in Wells, one wonders why he did not simply write a fuller study of Wells than was contained in his early doctoral dissertation. *Building the City of Man: Outlines of a World Civilization* is a rather weak book, which is filled more with trends from magazines than with visions from the future; and yet as an historian's attempt to deal with the primary fantasy of our time it is worth taking seriously.

The primary fantasy of our time is to escape catastrophe by building an ark or founding an apocalyptic colony far removed from the collapse of civilization. Only a few go to work with Soleri, because his arcologies remind most of us of the Tower of Babel and the Cities of the Plain, and we have been living in them for some time; but if Soleri were to build his arcologies deep under the Outback of Australia or under the ice of Antarctica, as Wagar would have him do, then thousands would line up two-by-two to fill the ark that was to save us from "the fire next time." If Soleri's *The City in the Image of Man* is a vision of the restructuring of urban civilization, Wagar's *Building the City of Man* is a more literal view of its destruction.

Wagar's emphasis on nuclear war gives his work a tragic outlook that is more open to religious modes of thought. Where Soleri sees the artistic culture of men as the unifying force of world civilization, Wagar recognizes the integrating power of the great universal religions:

At some point in its evolution, the ideology of world integration will find part of itself undergoing a rare and mysterious transfiguration; it will cease to be a merely deeply felt system of social values, or a program of social action; it will become a religion, from which—still later—may emerge the civil religion of the world republic. . . . We shall not reach, nor can we sustain, an organic world civilization, without the help of a new living religious faith.

But how does one "create" a new religion? Could a committee of venerable world religious leaders, or a team of sociologists of religion, or a battery of computers perform such a feat?[6]

The question is raised, but left unanswered, for Professor Wagar is willing to admit that "Scholars will probably have less to do with the making of a new world civilization than they would like to believe." Nevertheless, Professor Wagar, an historian at Harpur College in New York State, continues with his attempt to outline just such a civilization.

Wagar's book is a very strange one indeed; half of it is an incisive indictment of liberal and New Left pieties, and the other half is an invocation of exactly those forms of thought. Wagar successfully demonstrates the futile role the United Nations plays as just that kind of organization the powerful nation-states need to make certain that there will never be a world government. He sees that a leftist revolution in America which does not alter man's basically materialist orientation to nature, self, and society will only change the masks on the faces of those in power. And he sees the inanity of much self-congratulatory liberalism.

. . . the peace movement has tended to lose itself in narrow and doctrinaire byways. A movement whose only goal is peace (i.e., the absence of war) will never achieve it. One might as well start a happiness movement. Peace is the bliss and felicity that we may live to earn if we create a new world civilization; yet, in and of itself, it is nothing at all.[7]

Like so many of us, Wagar is best in criticism and weakest in his counterproposals. He calls for a world religion, but gives little indication of an understanding of the kind of experience from which religion springs. He approaches religion in the way a professor of creative writing approaches literature: as a basically rational experience that can be explained in the classroom. He indicts the peace movement and then calls for a world party movement that is nothing more than a global rerun of the "Come Clean with Gene" campaign of 1968.

The solution is difficult, but quite obvious. To bring into being an authentic world government, we must first bring into being an authentic world political party. . . .

In the bourgeois democracies, I would expect the world party to make its first appearance in a few large cities, as a coalition of exasperated liberals and radicals who can no longer function within the hopelessly compromised structures of the old leftist parties. The idea of a new world civilization may serve as a rallying cry of those liberals and radicals, but they will also represent the interests of oppressed or disadvantaged youth, women, the urban poor, together with a variety of alienated intellectuals.[8]

With the failure of the McCarthy campaign in 1968 and the McGovern campaign in 1972, liberal humanists like Wagar seem to be moving away from the old political dreams of the Adlai Stevenson era to new planetary fantasies. But one wonders how, if all the above movements could fail in the media-saturated society of the United States, such an international one would be able to bring Africa, Asia, and Latin America into its orbit. The very movement which saw itself as bringing world civilization to earth could bring the most intense forms of polarization imaginable. Certainly, the General Amins of the Third World would look upon it as nothing more than pretty packaging for the neo-imperialist designs of the white race.

But what is even more surprising about this scenario for the birth of a world party is that a futurist should choose to think in terms of a "party" in the first place. Clearly, the failures of the McCarthy and McGovern campaigns should point up the futility of regarding political parties as chosen instruments to effect the cultural evolution of the human race. Parties are national bureaucracies whose whole meaning is in organization first and philosophy second; this is one reason that John Lindsay or John Connally can switch from one party to another without creating a fuss. The party system is rooted in the city-country split of the nineteenth century, and its atavism is vividly expressed every four years in that nineteenth-century ritual, the convention. The new decentralizing informational technology is going to spell the end of the city-country split and the party system just as surely as television spelled an end to the photojournalism of *Life* magazine. The fact that we still live in an age of political parties and automobiles is no guarantee that a coming world civilization will take these instruments and magnify them on a planetary scale.

Thus the first step toward creating a world civilization should be, not the creation of a world party bureaucracy, but the separation of cultural authority from the parties by not using them for the things that will really matter in the culture of the future. In this way the political parties of the future will become as half-filled as the churches are now.

In his heart of hearts, Wagar realizes the futility of dreaming of such a linear, step-by-step campaign toward a planetary White House. Like a Herman Kahn, he thus prepares a few scenarios to show other, more "realistic" disasters:

Yet, let us not build our hypothetical castles too high. My guess is that long before the world party can overwhelm the nation-state system, perhaps before it mundializes a single country, a great war will erupt that will alter the world situation drastically. . . . In the wake of such a war, the conscience of the species will be badly bruised and unusually vulnerable to the arguments of the world party and its leaders. If the world party then has sufficient strength, it might seize power in one or more of the stricken combatant nations, taking advantage of temporary dislocations in normal political and economic life.[9]

In order to be certain that the world party has sufficient strength to emerge as a new force for world order, Wagar suggests that the party take out some "Doomsday insurance" now:

I suggest quite seriously that one fragment of the world revolutionary movement should detach itself from the main body at a very early stage and direct its energies toward the building of an ark of civilization, a renewal colony well enough staffed and supplied to guide the survivors of a total war back to civilized life and forward to human unity. . . . Building such a colony and keeping its facilities and personnel up to date would involve an initial investment of, let us say, $200,000,000, and yearly expenditures of $40,000,000—the cost of a medium-sized state university.[10]

The renewal colony is obviously Wagar's dream; you can see his imagination begin to take off, figuring out a budget, planning possible locations, and pondering "The Shape of Things to Come."

H. G. Wells played with many different scenarios for the rise of a world state, but the one that is closest to Wagar's renewal colony is also the one most widely known through Wells's film *The Shape of Things to Come*. In this film Wells shows the world of 1933 heading into an apocalypse brought on by the modern air warfare of the nations. Wave after wave of war washes over Europe until all resources and knowledge are consumed and the world collapses into another Dark Age. But somehow to the side of the madness a group of engineers and scientists has been able to escape and develop a superior technology in secret. When the tidal wave of the Great War has subsided and only eddying pools of tribal warfare remain, the engineers emerge from hiding and conquer the world with "the gas of peace." They call themselves "Wings Over the World" and represent "the freemasonary of science."

Both Wells and his student Wagar are in harmony in their pastoral vision of science in this ark of the new covenant. In this perfect renewal colony there will be no conflict, no politics, no problems that cannot be solved by the problem-solvers; all will agree on the good, all will see the good in the same way, and all will choose to act for the good with the same methods. Like B. F. Skinner, Wagar feels that if only greedy businessmen, ambitious politicians, and redneck constituents can be gotten out of the way, enlightened men of science will rule wisely and well. One can excuse Wells, for he lived long before the age of massive higher education; but one would think that academics who have lived in universities and observed the wisdom, goodness, and high ideals of their colleagues in the storied halls of learning would know better. But Wagar's colony is not so much a place as a pastoral, an imaginary realm free of conflict that one dreams about while he is suffering from all the agonies of the permanent contradictions of human nature.

No political movement can save us from the human condition that values are achieved in conflict with their opposites. The politics of the renewal colony will be no different from the politics of the university or the church. At least in his science fiction vision of dark ages and a renewal colony, *Foundation*, Isaac Asimov is willing to be realistic about the inevitability of problems with the solution.

But since a vision of a renewal colony is one of the primary fantasies of our time, let us go further into it and give it the benefit of more doubts than one. Since all states, corporations, universities, foundations, and churches are locked into the present system of industrial nation-states, they cannot be expected to be the sources of funds for the colony. We must look to some imaginative billionaire, so let us imagine that we have found a Howard Hughes who in his old age wants to become the savior of mankind by funding such a colony. The first problem with funds will be the funder: if he has the imagination to play the role of planetary savior, he will not likely have the humility to turn over his leadership to a committee of technocrats. Most likely he will want to be the savior of civilization in as lively a way as possible— much to the annoyance of the scientists who have cut themselves adrift from civilization with him. But let us not shipwreck the ark too soon. Let us assume even further that the funder is willing not only to give the money but also to give up his power to the scientists. The next problem will be the scientists: Which scientists? B. F. Skinner with his behavioral reinforcements? José Delgado with his electronic stimulation of the brain? Or R. K. Wallace with his Transcendental Meditation? If we appoint only scientists of one group, we are likely to get a leader with his mediocre following, but if we appoint scientists of different groups, we are sure to get conflict. One must remember that when there is conflict in a university, an individual can always quit and go to another university, but in the renewal colony there is, by definition, no place else to go.

For the sake of fantasy, let us push on beyond these initial disappointments. Let us suppose that the various subgroups of the scientists don't come into conflict with one another, that the sociologists agree with the psychologists, and that the practical engineers agree with the theoretical physicists. We now assume that we have funded the colony and that it is working beautifully. The next problem is how to hide this conspiracy for taking over the world. If one were to sneak the colony into Latin America, he would run the risk of generating paranoid fantasies that the CIA was using the colony as a cover operation for some scientific dirty work too dangerous to carry on in the U.S.A. The natives would be likely to get upset that they were being used as guinea pigs by the gringos, and like the Transylvanian villagers attacking the castle of the good Dr. Frankenstein, the whole place would be likely to be burnt down in short order. So we will have to put it in the Outback of Australia or under the ice of Antarctica. But how is one going to sneak in several IBM computers and all the other $100 million worth of technical equipment without the CIA or the Russians wondering what is going on? The nation-states will have paranoid fantasies of the Mafia building a thermonuclear planetary blackmail base, and, God knows, the Mafia are about the only ones who could afford to build Wagar's colony. Before you know it, Russian and American spy satellites will be bleeping overhead and the very attempt to make the colony secret will make it the most discussed project in the world.

If one makes the planetary scientific project public, it is doomed to surveillance and interference; if one makes it private, it is doomed to even greater surveillance and interference. Obviously, the best strategy would be to make the renewal colony out in the open, but with a psychological cover that gave it perfect protection. As a matter of fact, this is exactly what Father Noah did: he just started right in to build his ark hundreds of miles from the sea—to the delight of all his neighbors. So, if one could find a way to violate the reality of society so outrageously (but sanely) that one were not taken seriously, he might stand a chance of hiding the conspiracy for world takeover. If the renewal colony is to be left in peace by the governments of America and Russia, it must be purely nonscientific and crankily religious. But if it is crankily religious, it cannot work at all on Wells's or Wagar's terms.

In the final analysis, Wagar's scheme simply won't work. The only possible good that could come out of the world party with its renewal colony would be if Russia and the United States decided to gang up on the world party to form a planetary alliance and beat it to the punch. But I'm sure that it wouldn't take a renewal colony to accomplish this;

the idea has probably already occurred to Nixon and Brezhnev at their last summit meeting. But if the Soviet Union and the United States are going to push the world around into some kind of order, then one wants the United States to be in some kind of decent shape itself. What kind of shape would it be in if every good scientist, scholar, artist, and New Age man were off in the Outback of Australia or under the ice of Antarctica?

Planting a scientific renewal colony away from civilization would aggravate the split in mankind. Since an increase in information generates an increase in entropy elsewhere in the system (libraries destroy forests), it is likely that a leap upward to a new informational class contained in the colony would generate an increase in entropy in humanity. Homo Sapiens would become the new Neanderthals to the new scientific Cro-Magnons, and the colony would stimulate the very destruction it was designed to forestall.

But if we abandon the prospects of escaping to a colony, the prospects for fixing up the world on its own terms are not very bright. Some thinkers, like Arnold Toynbee, think that we have no other choice than a planetary dictatorship:

As I look back on the social history of past ages, I do fear that, in the present state of the world, the establishment of a dictatorial world state in the style of the Akkadian, Persian, Roman, and Chinese Empires is the most probable development. . . .

I can imagine the world being held together and kept at peace in the year 2000 by an atrociously tyrannical dictatorship which would not hesitate to kill or torture anyone who, in its eyes, was a menace to the unquestioning acceptance of its absolute authority. . . .

If I am right about this, I daresay that one of the propaganda devices that the coming world tyranny might use, in the hope of reducing this regime's unpopularity, would be to commission the writing of Utopias drawing idealized pictures of past attempts at establishing something like world governments. . . .

If the reluctant majority does accept this dictatorship on this ground, I think they will be making the right choice, because it would enable the human race to survive.[11]

Professor Wagar is, of course, not calling for any of these horrors to accompany his world state, and given his own prophecies of "sexual Samaritanism," it is more likely that his world state would rule through pleasure than through torture, but it is clear that he is not calling enough of human nature into account in his prescription for world order. He fails to see that by the usual *enantidromias* of human nature his very dream of a world party is likely to become Toynbee's nightmare. Wagar's arguments are precisely those the world state would use to rationalize its own existence. If the university intellectuals who directed Presidents Kennedy and Johnson's ventures in Vietnam are any indication, the intellectuals on salary in the universities will make their peace with the world state in short order.

While it tightens its structures of world consolidation, the regime will buy off the secular intelligentsia by apparent concessions to civil liberties in the form of sexual liberation. Wagar's naïveté is clearly in evidence in this area in his *Playboy* approach to the role of sexuality in contemporary culture. He sees the future of sexuality in terms borrowed from the early Marcuse and not the later Marcuse of "repressive desublimation."

We may expect the rise of what Lars Ullerstam has called a "sexual Samaritanism," a new class of volunteer social workers who love mankind well enough to provide sexual services for those least able to negotiate liaisons by themselves.[12]

Just as Wagar adopts the bankrupt party system for his world movement, so he adopts the ghastly system of abusive social work for his ideal republic. Wagar would do well to remember the Goncourt brothers' remark on the role of pornography in the state: "One tames people as one tames lions, by masturbation." It is disappointing to see that when an academic historian tries to turn futurist, the best he can do for us is the civil religion of a world state, a new political party, and Playmate social workers.

Whether Wagar wants his world party and renewal colony to have only good guys in it or not, it is likely to move into its opposite very quickly. And what if there are two renewal colonies, one using Skinnerian social science and another using countercultural religion? How will we deal with conflict between different renewal colonies, each absolutely convinced that it holds the true answer to the predicament of mankind, if we no longer have the traditions of constitutional law to protect science and religion from one another? Perhaps we should remember that America started out as a renewal colony. In Plymouth Plantation, the Pilgrims who had left the Old World behind were full of a new spirit of love and were at peace with the Indians of the New World; but by the time their grandchildren had taken over the colony, the peace with the Indians was broken in the very first of the American Vietnams, King Philip's War.

Professor Wagar is a former World Federalist and a present contributor to the Institute for World Order, but all the contributors to the Institute are not of a single mind with him. The German contributor takes a much more skeptical attitude toward these fantasies of scientific world government, and he is much more able to speak on the role of science in the government of the world; for he lived through one of those historical moments when international science and national politics became critically related. Professor C. F. von Weizsäcker is now the Director of the Max Planck Institute for Research into the Conditions of Life in the Scientific and Technical World in Starnberg, Germany. Internationally recognized for his achievements in physics and astrophysics, Weizsäcker, like Heisenberg and Lorenz, is the German (and much more formal) equivalent of the individual as institution in that he has his own institute in the Max Planck Society. Professor von Weizsäcker's career has had an interesting development, first as a physicist, then as Professor of Philosophy at Hamburg, and now as a social scientist directing a research institute on the future of the technological society. But perhaps his past is even more interesting than his present, for he is credited by some historians as being one of the three men who helped keep the atom bomb out of Hitler's hands.

Houtermans, despite his own political peril, naturally got into direct communication with Heisenberg and Weizsäcker, soon after his release by the Gestapo. He wanted to learn from their own lips just what the object of the Uranium Society was. He received the consoling information that every effort was to be concentrated on the problem of a "uranium machine" with the intention of progressively diverting the attention of the government from the possibility of the bomb. . . .

It seems paradoxical that the German nuclear physicists, living under a saber-rattling dictatorship, obeyed the voice of conscience and attempted to prevent the construction of atom bombs, while their professional colleagues in the democracies, who had no coercion to fear, with very few exceptions concentrated their whole energies on the production of the new weapon.[13]

When I visited Professor von Weizsäcker in his office in a tower overlooking Lake Starnberg, I reminded him of H. G. Wells's "Wings Over the World" scenario for the takeover by the "freemasonry of science," and asked him whether he thought there was a chance that a Pythagorean Brotherhood of Scientists could work in secret to direct the drift of civilization away from disaster. He had been talking in a rather general way a moment before, but at the mention of the word "Pythagorean" his eyes darted back from the window and he stared at me with testing, inquiring eyes. He became more interested and his face took on a more youthful and lively spirit, and then he began to reminisce about the last great encounter between the mysteries of science and the power of the state.

Weizsäcker said that before the war he had had an idea that he now knew to be naïve, but that at the time he had thought could work. If the dozen or more members of the club of atomic science, those very few who were initiate to the inner mysteries, could be convinced to take a secret vow to keep atomic physics out of the hands of all national politicians, then a great disaster could be averted. Weizsäcker said he mentioned this idea to Heisenberg and that they discussed it thoroughly. And then they made a decision that he now sees was foolish and a clear mistake: they decided that in order to be certain that there was indeed a danger to atomic science and that it all wasn't a chimerical fantasy, they would have to do the research. If they found that their fears were not unfounded and that there really was a possibility of atomic weapons, then they could close in over the secret and keep it to themselves. How Faustian it all appeared to me. The scientists were tempted deeper into danger by their own irresistible desire to know; what made them great as scientists was a trait that had become a tragic flaw.

Their strategy was simple in idea but difficult in execution. On the advice of the aged Max Planck,[14] Werner Heisenberg declined positions in America and returned to Nazi Germany in the hopes of keeping German science alive after the inevitable defeat of Hitler. When Heisenberg's former student, Weizsäcker, was assigned to his laboratory, the two decided to work together to convince the government to take other young physicists out of the army and into the laboratory. Since atomic physics was looked upon as "Jewish physics" by the Nazis, it was difficult to convince them of the merit of their project without dangerously overconvincing them with the prospect of atomic weapons. Their strategy was to make a case for the feasibility of atomic power and the infeasibility of atomic weapons. By setting up the diversionary movement of the "Uranium Society," they hoped to save the lives of their best young scientists and throw the government off the track. Since funds were scarce there was little likelihood that the government would grant them millions with an ultimatum to build an atomic bomb, and both Heisenberg and Weizsäcker felt that it would be technically impossible to build such a weapon under wartime conditions anyway. Weizsäcker did not believe it was even possible to build one in wartime America. A European aristocrat who believes in letting things take their slow and natural growth, Weizsäcker would be instinctively suspicious of the value of the crash projects of American bureaucratic science. More interested in Plato than in Manhattan or Apollo projects, Weizsäcker is willing to admit: "We spent two million; you spent two billion. And that was that."

Once the German physicists felt secure from the threat of a German atomic bomb, their greatest worry was that a bomb might be dropped on Germany. Weizsäcker suggested that Heisenberg assure his old teacher, Niels Bohr, that the Allies need have no fear of a German bomb. On a visit to Copenhagen, Heisenberg tried to give those assurances; but he spoke in such a guarded manner that at the mere mention of the bomb Bohr panicked, mistook his meaning, and with the bitterness of the Nazi occupation of Denmark before him, went back to convince the Allies of the absolute necessity of beating the Germans to the punch.

All in all, when one takes into consideration the extremely complicated politics of science contained in the lessons of World War II, it is difficult to have much faith that a group of scientists could save the world. When I described to Weizsäcker Wagar's proposal for a renewal colony, he disagreed with its feasibility. "If they have any superior science

that constitutes a threat to the nations, they will be killed."
He also felt that it would be impossible to achieve unanimity
in the colony, and explained that not all conflicts between
scientists were simply patriotic ones. He pointed out that his
good friend Edward Teller was no patriot, but a man who
simply felt that the greatest menace to the world was world
Communism; to check this threat he felt it was absolutely
necessary that America be given the hydrogen bomb. Oppenheimer, on the other hand, was already suffering like a Greek
tragic hero, and felt that enough sins had been committed in
giving the politicians the atom bomb.

Conflict or betrayal would be inevitable in a colony. There
had been intense rivalry between Oppenheimer and Teller,
and out of that personal power race had come another spurt
of energy for the arms race. If individuals like Klaus Fuchs
could always be found to give away national secrets, un-
doubtedly just as many could be found to give away the
secrets of the Pythagorean Brotherhood.

As I left Weizsäcker's office, I was struck by the moral
ambiguities contained in that tragic moment of history. One
could not write a play with greater ironies. We Americans
tend to look upon Einstein as a saint, but his letter to FDR
produced a chain reaction that ended up in the incineration
of Hiroshima and Nagasaki. Many Americans regard Heisenberg and Weizsäcker as culpable because they did not come
to America along with Fermi and Teller. They chose not to
abandon their culture, but to follow Max Planck's advice
to build a renewal colony right in the middle of the Nazi
state. Because they worked for dictators, they did not believe
in their own government, and thus no Hiroshima or Dresden
can be laid at the doorstep of German physics. Because the
American scientists believed in their government, they were
fooled into entrusting their authority into the hands of power;
out of that trust came the takeover by the state of American
higher education. In fighting them, America became like the

militarist regimes of Japan and Germany, and thus proved the wisdom of the Hindu maxim "We become what we hate."

How much easier it would have been for Heisenberg to stay in the United States, and how much harder it was to return to Germany. As an American who had left the country in the summer of assassinations in 1968 to go to Canada, I knew the other side of emigration and did not feel so confident as the critics of Heisenberg and Weizsäcker that they were guilty by location.[15]

I came away from my conversation with Weizsäcker deeply impressed and more firmly convinced than ever that there could be no secret renewal colony. Science had to be kept out in the open and held up to scrutiny and moral judgment from all sides of human culture. If we are ever to have a confederation of nations, each affirming individual civil liberties, those liberties are not likely to develop out of the soil of a secret and conspiratorial scientific society.

But the secret "freemasonry of science" was not the only approach to world government that Wells had in mind. At the moment, the "Open Conspiracy" seems to be more with us in the work of a group of men that Wells would approve of, the Club of Rome. It was a few weeks after the publication of the Club of Rome's "Project on the Predicament of Mankind," *The Limits to Growth*,[16] that I returned to MIT to talk with its chief author, Dennis Meadows. His office was in an old converted factory building that I had passed many times on the way to the Faculty Club when I was teaching at MIT; but then I did not know that Jay Forrester was teaching a group of young computer scientists, of whom Meadows was one, how to put the planet into a model. The model which Forrester had developed for the city,[17] and which had been so roundly trounced by even the RAND Corporation for its total failure to express the complex reality of the city,[18] was now about to be extended to the whole world. As I went up the stairs in the old factory warehouse, I thought it was fitting that in a castoff factory a group of men was describing the end to the age of factories and the growth of industrial society.

While I waited in the outside office to see Meadows I had time to glance over all the press clippings on *The Limits to Growth* which covered the bulletin board on one wall. The clippings gave the place the atmosphere of a campaign office, and I wondered who was running for what. When I went in to see Meadows, he seemed distracted, as if he were being interrupted in the middle of some rather serious business. It was clear that I would not have much time, so I decided I had better get in my questions fast. Meadows leaned back, put his Sahara boots up on his desk, and for a moment in his casual corduroys appeared to be more a young Harvard instructor of English than an MIT computer scientist. He told me that the book was being published simultaneously in a dozen or more languages, and it was obvious that all this international-public-affairs business was quite a change from his computering. I wanted to know more about the cultural implications of the Club of Rome, but Meadows did not seem happy with these questions and said that I should talk to Peccei—if I could find him sitting still in one place long enough. Meadows said that he had joined the Club reluctantly, and only because it was easier to do his work inside its network of information and communication. He did not want to be a global jet-setter who went around giving discourses on the collapse of the industrial system.

"If there isn't that much time left for civilization, I don't see the point of wasting what's left running around spending your life in airports. I'm leaving MIT and going to teach at Dartmouth and live on a farm. With three or four graduate students, I will have the only kind of exponential growth I'm interested in."

I decided I would try one more question concerning the

cultural implications of the Club of Rome, and since time was running short, I loaded up a ponderous one.

"If we accept your idea that we are coming to a period of limits being placed on industrial development, doesn't that mean that we are reaching the limits to 'The Protestant Ethic and the Spirit of Capitalism,' and the old capitalist market economy, and shifting to a neomercantilist one where some crowning agency will have to grant charters to new Planetary Hudson Bay Companies to husband our dwindling resources? But what agency is going to limit the huge multinationals? In the days of the competing empires, the Papacy was used to create a Line of Demarcation to split the New World between Catholic Spain and Portugal. What agency do you see overlooking the husbanding of the world's resources, saying so much oil for Japan, so much for Western Europe, but, to preserve the atmospheric oxygen produced by the Amazon basin, only very limited oil for Brazil?"

"You know," Meadows answered, "it's pretty hard to carry on a conversation with you. You're talking on several tracks at once. But if you're getting at a world state, I don't think that would be a good idea. It would be monolithic and bureaucratic, and since there would be no government external to it, it couldn't help but become tyrannical."

"But isn't some form of world management implicit in everything the Club of Rome is doing? Aren't you *really* saying, 'Look, if we can manage to put the planet into a model, you can be sure that we could come up with some model for planetary management'?"

"You're going to have to talk to Peccei."

And so, I realized, I would.

H. G. Wells once belonged to a dining club called "The Coefficients"; the group included such distinguished men as J. B. S. Haldane, Bertrand Russell, and Sydney Webb.[19] They would meet once a month to discuss the affairs of the Empire.

And there, no doubt, Wells had numerous opportunities to make the case for his world order, whether it was to be the "New Republicans," the "Order of the Samurai," or "Wings Over the World." One can see the port decanter, the dinner jackets, and the cigar smoke, and recall just how close the British Empire did come to being a planetary world state. The Club of Rome is very much in the tradition of the Coefficients, and its founder, Aurelio Peccei, would be perfect at such a gathering. In fact, when I finally did have an occasion to talk with Peccei, he openly expressed his wish that we were living under the British rather than the American Empire.

It was in the office of his own consulting firm, Italconsult, in the suburbs of Rome, that I met Peccei for the first time. I was lucky, for tomorrow he would be in Japan, and after that, who knew where? And yet Peccei nowhere showed that he was in a rush. He did not know me from Adam, but was quite willing to stop and have a conversation about the Club of Rome. And so we sat at the conference table in his office, sipped espresso, and talked about the end of the world.

Peccei is a distinguished-looking man of medium height and slightly thick but solid build; with his white hair and mustache, he has more the air of a statesman than a business-man, and, perhaps, that statesman's sensibility is the reason he could not rest with his directorships of Olivetti, Fiat, and Alitalia, but had to move out to the sphere of global man-agement. In an American this restlessness might express itself as a subtle underlying anxiety and compensatory drive, but Peccei has all the outer balance and composure of a Euro-pean. With a Gaullist combination of humanism and technoc-racy, Peccei feels that only Europe can come between the clumsy giants of America and Russia to lead the world to better things than war or ecological suicide.

Let's see if this huge, complex equation can be put through our minds and then our computers. And who is better able to start

this human venture than we Europeans? The Russians can't, because they are not an open society. The Americans can't take the
initiative because there is little credibility in the United States
and probably there is not this deep-seated heritage of culture, of
tradition, of world-wiseness that there is in Europe. Let's see if
we Europeans can render this great service to mankind—now
that we have come together. To conceive a new world, and to
start with a blueprint for managing the world equitably and to its
fullest capacities. Are we capable of this? I think we are.[20]

In conversation, Peccei was clearer about his distaste for
the vulgar energy of America, its lack of culture, its disorder.
Of course, he made me understand, he had his ambivalences;
half of him was deeply involved in the States and his son even
went to Stanford. One could see why Peccei and ecology had
come together: America was uncontrolled energy, pouring
out pollution and takeovers of European companies and
culture. His vision might be planetary, but his voice was the
neo-Gaullist voice of old Europe, of grace, of balance, of
energy restrained and held in the form of simple but assured
elegance. In looking for a world civilization Peccei was also
looking in a mirror for a dynamic form which could create
a civilization, but still rest poised and modest. If his values
were put to work in the ecosystem, then perhaps the earth
would have half a century more than it would have in the
clumsy hands of the Americans.

Peccei's talk of the British Empire impressed me, for only
a month before in India I had listened to Gopi Krishna speak
fondly of the British and claim how much better things had
been under them. "When they followed their own laws and
arrested even Lords guilty of graft, they were unconquerable;
but when later they became decadent and lax and allowed
corruption to go unchecked, the Empire was ruined." Gopi
Krishna had spent a career as a clerk in a provincial government office, so it was understandable that his sense of order
would be offended at sloppy, modern India; but it was doubly

impressive to hear the Kashmiri clerk and the Italian corporation president speak in similar ways about the moral basis of empire. I had only studied the underside of the British Empire in Ireland, and the picture there was anything but one of dedicated public servants following the great traditions of English law. And yet when one looked at General Amin in Uganda and Ian Smith in Rhodesia, one wondered if the brilliant Julius Nyerere of Tanzania could make up the balance. But perhaps Gopi Krishna's hindsight is the only way an empire can be made to seem attractive.

Since Peccei seemed to see the positive side of the British Empire, I wondered if he saw the multinational corporations as equally attractive empires. Having seen Coca-Cola signs written in Amharic, and having seen the Communist Chinese Agricultural Mission to Ethiopia drinking Coca-Cola's "Fanta" at dinner, I had begun to wonder if the sun ever set on a Coca-Cola sign. But Pececi's answer was direct and startling.

"There is no such thing as a multinational corporation. No one, for example, really thinks that Ford is a multinational corporation."

Peccei's answer was rather surprising when one considered that he was a member of the Board of Directors for Olivetti-Underwood, but perhaps his experience with Fiat in Latin America had been more instructive about Ford. He seemed to hold little faith in the managers of the multinationals and looked to them not for a new and imaginative form of planetary leadership but rather for a race to gobble up the world's resources. Peccei felt that the politician and the businessman were both nearsighted and could not see beyond their most powerful constituencies. The world needed a different kind of man. The artist could see, he claimed, no doubt because he knew I was in humanities and probably felt he had been a bit heavy-handed on the Americans. But I matched his attack on the businessman with an attack on the artist and said that most modern novelists or gallery painters suffered from the same myopia as the businessman. But Peccei had the old European vision of "The Artist," and had not taken a closer look at some of them for a long time.

"But if you value art, why are there no artistic or religious visionaries in your Club of Rome? Why only technocrats, businessmen, diplomats, and government officials?"

"We are interested in going beyond descriptions to solutions. We wish to recognize new policy guidelines and organize patterns to manage the human lot intelligently, and to foster their implementation."

Peccei picked up on my mention of religion and said that he felt there was a role the Vatican and the Church could take in planetary affairs, which was certainly the last thing I had in mind when I spoke of "religious visionaries."

As our conversation neared its close, I thought how little of Peccei's style and force showed through in his book, *The Chasm Ahead.*[21] As a man of Europe repelled by vulgar America, it was strange how he had become in the book a prisoner of American think-tank banalities, phony management sciences, and the pseudo social science of Zbigniew Brzezinski. Like Ivan Illich, Peccei is a man who is really not expressed in books, and that is, no doubt, why one had his CIDOC and the other his Club of Rome.

Peccei had said that he was not familiar with the work of H. G. Wells; nevertheless, Peccei and the Club were the very men Wells had been waiting for. So why not let them take over? Peccei was an impressive man of good will, and that was certainly more than one could say for Nixon, Brezhnev, Heath, or Pompidou. Would the mess these new men get us into be any worse than the mess we were in?

The most socially influential description of the mess we are in is, of course, provided by the Club of Rome itself. Here are men coming out of the bastions of prestige who ignore the clogged conduits of power in the national governments and the United Nations and finesse the whole situation by setting up their own institution of instant authority. Since they are sitting there cornering the market on global disasters, where can we go to buy disaster insurance but to the great ones who first pointed out the danger to us? In order to solve problems on a planetary scale, we have to use the problem-solving devices they are putting into our hands. Like a member of an audience who rises to ask a question he has already answered in the elaborate question, the Club of Rome is the explicit formulation of a problem in which it implicitly figures as the solution.

There are, of course, disclaimers. Like a candidate who officially begins his campaign by making a public announcement that he will not be a candidate under any circumstances, the Club of Rome has covered itself on that score.

. . . it must be repeated that the Club of Rome seeks no political role and will not advocate policies. It restricts its function to assisting in the elucidation of the world problematique and in bringing its analyses to the attention of policy makers who alone, responsive to the opinions of the people, must decide.[22]

All of which is as prudent as it is nonsensical, for how can the people decide on the validity of Forrester's and Meadows's computer models and projections? Whether an astrologer or an MIT computer scientist stands at the right hand of the king, the omens of the final days cannot be read by the multitude.

One can see why the parliamentary monarchy of the British Empire appeals to Peccei. Having spent a year in the Italian Fascist prisons, he is no lover of dictatorship and abhors as much as anything else its debasement of human culture. The more civilized traditions of a ruling class open to upward mobility would be more attractive to Peccei. If the multitude has been excluded from the Club of Rome, it is because the Club is a group of men of influence, and men of influence are by definition not in the multitude.

In and of itself there is nothing inherently wrong with elitism. Democracy is invoked, not because it is better than elitism (for no one would deny that the achievements of the world's great cities and cultural movements have come from the synergistic effect of bringing geniuses together), but because the traditions of democratic constitutional law provide the best protection for elites, from themselves as much as from the people. And we greatly oversimplify society if we think that there is one homogeneous group called the best that is waiting to be sifted from the mass. There are many elites, and they have been coming into conflict with one another throughout history. As soon as a planetary elite was established in a world state, a revolutionary elite would form against it. This is true not only for government or science but for religion as well.

If we truly wish to achieve a planetary transformation of human culture, we must go beyond the authoritarian conspiracies of Wells and Wagar and the technocratic elitism of the Club of Rome to raise into consciousness the cosmic mythologies that are now sweeping over the planet. We do not need any more "politics" than we already have. The historical contribution to planetary culture of the American Revolution was to create all the politics we would need, in the words of the Masonic Great Seal on the back of the dollar bill, for the "Novus Ordo Seclorum." If we have another Russian or Chinese Revolution in which the individual is compressed into being a unit in the mass, we will lose the unique opening to the universal that is contained in the self. Only through this microcosmic opening can the macrocosmic energies flood in to give us the art, science, and religion of a new Renaissance. Through stepping down the energies of the individual by consolidating him with the Total State, we will, ironically, aggravate our problems by eliminating the imagination with which we could solve them. As the instant political solutions turn into new problems, the state will have to introduce control after control to replace the old moral traditions until society is a nightmare of mechanized system and chaos. System and chaos are linked opposites, just as morality and freedom are. Try to create a system by which nations deliver each other's mail, and watch the chaos result; give up system and let each nation *trust* the other to *respect* its postage and deliver its mail, and watch the order unfold.

Modern man likes to think that he has outgrown the age of morality and has replaced it with positivistic social science, but if each time we drove a car, the wheels fell off because the mechanic didn't *care*, or each time we talked to someone, he *lied* to us, society would stop at once. The positivists would be thrown out, and the next day people would go back to a moralistic way of looking at things.

The theologian Bultmann, and the sociologist Weber have characterized the modern post-Christian era as one of de-mythologizing and disenchantment. But secularization is merely a temporary and very necessary process to give new energies to the sacred and to release it from the prison of the old forms. The sacred is greater than the sacerdotal. The Pharisees keep up their costumes and are careful with whom they associate, but Jesus travels with whores and tramps. If we look around us in contemporary culture, we no longer see the world of Bultmann and Weber, but one of planetary remythologizing and re-enchantment. These energetic trans-formations, however, are not coming from the elite culture of the scientific academies of Wagar or the board rooms of the members of the Club of Rome; they are coming from popular culture. *The Limits to Growth* brazenly calls "for a fundamental revision in human behavior and, by implication, of the entire fabric of present-day society,"[23] but nowhere do these MIT men realize that a true re-*vision*ing of human culture is already going on.

What is a nonpolluting, non-Faustian, nongrowth Western culture going to look like? The people who have been doing the Research and Development on this new culture are not at MIT, but in the new popular counterculture. If this attitude seems fanciful, one should stop to consider that all our technological solutions are only contributing to the "problematique." There is no way that industrial society, Chinese or American, can solve the problem of industrial society; it is locked into a double-bind in which all its quick "fixes" and solutions are negative feedback loops to nature and culture. Antipollution devices increase fuel consumption and inflation, which increase America's economic instability and dependence on Arabian oil, which increases Arab ambitions, which increases Israel's nervous defensiveness, which increases the likelihood of Armageddon.

Though the resources of industrial society may be shrinking, the spiritual resources of nature are cosmically expanding for planetary society. The people of the new culture realize that if we are going to humanize technology, we will need more than the *New York Review of Books;* if we are going to have a fundamental revision of human behavior, we will need more than MIT or the Club of Rome; if we are going to have more than a World Total State, we will need more than a political revolution. At the end of the line for industrial society, we discover that it's a spiral and that we have turned and are now facing back in the direction of cosmic mythology. Now all the old maps take on a new meaning as they warn us, "Here be dragons." Ecstasy *or* economics, madness *or* sanity, mysticism *or* science: where ancient dragons live modern categories die.

FIVE

Of Physics and Tantra Yoga

"I have always felt that it is better to be esoteric from within society than esoteric in some mysterious place hidden away in the Himalayas." As he mused in his tower overlooking the Starnbergersee, Professor von Weizsäcker seemed to be summing up his whole career. The latest act in that career is certainly in keeping with that conviction. Having established a Max Planck Institute for the study of the technological society, he has gone on to create a private Research Foundation for Eastern Wisdom and Western Science. Out of a friendship that developed with the Kashmiri yogi, Gopi Krishna, Weizsäcker has gathered together a small group of German scientists interested in research and intellectual exploration at the interface between East and West.

The wedding of the mystique of German science and the mysticism of Indian yoga evokes all the archetypal images of an alchemical marriage; as you hear rumors of mysterious happenings in Starnberg, you go over expecting to see the salamander in the flames. Before I had gone to Germany, I had heard rumors from graduate students that the German physicists were conducting esoteric research with Gopi

Krishna. Legend had it that when they would photograph him, he would irradiate the film so that only an outline of light would show up in the picture. But the American graduate students were simply projecting; the research that was going on with Swami Rama at the Menninger Institute in Kansas was being distorted into a science fiction film, and for that film German physicists were much more cinematic than Midwestern doctors. When I arrived in Starnberg, I discovered that one of the members of Weizsäcker's Research Foundation had taken a few EEG measurements of Gopi Krishna in meditation, but that there was no research being conducted on the scale of Wallace's work at Harvard or Kamiya's work at Langley Porter. Weizsäcker himself thought it silly to look upon the Research Foundation as anything more than a club, a *"Verein."* As we talked in his office, our conversation was drawn more in the direction of Wagar, Wells, and the Club of Rome than to the scientific explanation of yoga. What Weizsäcker had to say about yoga was in his introduction to Gopi Krishna's essay on kundalini.

But what Weizsäcker had to say about science, world affairs, and atomic research in Hitler's Germany was so fascinating that I almost forgot I had flown over to Germany to meet Gopi Krishna and the physicists around him. When I did meet Gopi Krishna later that day, the meeting was something of an anticlimax. Nothing could be further from the truth of Gopi Krishna's simple and unassuming manner than the American legends of initiatic wonder-working. To appreciate how normal Gopi Krishna is, you have to set him against a theatrical guru like Sri Chinmoy. When you go to see Sri Chinmoy, you come upon a resplendent figure in gold slippers and saffron robes. With his eyeballs rolled up and his lips curled into a blissful smile of nirbikalpa samadhi, you do not have a conversation with him, you have darshan with an exalted being who uses more subtle vibrations than the pathetic beating of the wind with the larynx. If you stare at this being while he intones to his devotees, you will see a purple aura emanating from his head and shoulders. And if you look into the eyes of his disciples, you will see little reflections of Sri Chinmoy, their doorway to the infinite; and with his smile upon their lips, they will tell you that every morning they rise to meditate gazing upon the photograph of their master in samadhi. Since Sri Chinmoy was the only yogi I had ever talked to, I was prepared for darshan when I was ushered into Gopi Krishna's room in Starnberg.

But darshan it was not. Gopi Krishna rose from his desk, and in his white turban, the seventy-year-old fair-skinned Kashmiri stood tall and strongly present in a very physical way. With a warm and solicitous smile, he motioned me to a chair across from his little writing table. I sat down and looked into his bright and clear eyes and saw a grandfatherly goodness but no purple aura's majesty. His accent was Indian, and the dental sharpness of his speech was matched with a sharply didactic manner. He gave me little set-pieces and mini-lectures that answered questions I did not have and missed the questions I did have.

Months later, when I got to know him better on his own soil in Kashmir, I realized that his didactic approach was simply his defensive response to being questioned by academics. When he was relaxed and at home in Srinigar, he was warm, very friendly, and an avatar of Kashmiri hospitality. The cosmic theater of the kingly guru was missing, and the humble pride of Gopi Krishna struck me quite differently from the proud humility of Sri Chinmoy. The overall impression he created was one of goodness. Gopi Krishna was a good man, a family patriarch and a village pandit, but not another god-man of the Himalayas. If you were to translate the government clerk from Kashmir into American culture, you would come up with a working-class sage: an old logger from the Northwest with a love for books or a wizened and storied fisherman from Maine. As you questioned him about other yogis and other yogic traditions, you could see that, so much like a working-class sage, he was suspicious and felt that the famous yogis often did not know what it was all about. Like an Eric Hoffer or an H. G. Wells, Gopi Krishna had all the virtues and vices of a self-made man: free of authority figures, he was bound to his own brand of authoritarianism. After meditating on his own for fourteen years, he had discovered a physiological basis to religion and genius in the experience of the raising of kundalini. Now he could climb to higher levels of religious contemplation or go into an artistic trance to write 150 pages of rhyming poetry effortlessly.

Gopi Krishna is especially pleased with his new poetic gifts; and the fact that he can receive and transmit poetry written in languages he does not know convinces him of the quality of genius of this creative process. It is, perhaps, unfair to quote his poetry, but since he does claim that Kundalini Yoga is responsible for his transformation from an ordinary civil servant into a poet and sage of a new era of human evolution, the poetry must be taken into account.

> Those who adrift in fancy's golden realm
> Of harsh reality let go the helm
> And floating smoothly down the gliding stream
> Of thought, of the hidden future try to dream,
> Most often build its image on the shape
> Of present-day conditions, hard to escape,
> On their likes and dislikes, choice and desire,
> Which often color mortals' thought entire,
> And thus let their minds be enfettered by
> So much of earth they lose sight of the sky,
> One day to wake up with a sudden start
> To find their dream-world falling all apart.

In the Vedic tradition sacred knowledge is always transmitted in verse; and in Sanskrit the vibrations of the words are pitched in harmony with the vibrations of the cosmos; thus all Indian saints feel compelled to give authority to their utterances by means of poetry. With millennia of tradition behind him, an Indian sage simply cannot resist the temptation to write poetry. Unfortunately, whether it is the poetry of Sri Aurobindo, Paramahansa Yogananda, Sri Chinmoy, or Pandit Gopi Krishna, it is an artistic embarrassment. Of course, you can forgive a yogi his bad verses, but when he eagerly offers his poetry as proof that yoga is good not only for the soul but for the IQ and artistic ability as well, you can only wonder why illumination isn't light enough to see the poetry for what it is. In trying to prove the worth of the East to the West, yogis often only prove their total lack of understanding of the West.

Gopi Krishna wants to offer scientific proof for the claims of yoga, and in this effort he is more likely to secure an audience by working with Weizsäcker than by writing alone. Yogis we have always had with us; physicists interested in yoga we have not had. The first expression of Weizsäcker and Gopi Krishna's collaboration in the Research Foundation for Eastern Wisdom and Western Science is the publication of a small volume, *The Biological Basis of Religion and Genius.*[1] Since the introduction by Weizsäcker is almost as long as the text itself, it is fair to look upon this book as a jointly authored work; certainly for most Westerners, it is the introduction that will arouse the greater interest.

If yogic physics seems to be an oxymoron, it is a figure of speech in a language that is now part of the traditions of German science. While our scientists are claiming to have cast a new cold and scientific light on man that resolves the ambiguous flesh tones into one ghastly pallor, the German physicists are pointing out that even the light of science still oscillates with a darkness we do not understand. In 1971 Heisenberg's *Physics and Beyond* appeared in English, and although Heisenberg is no yogi, his views on God and the "central order" would not positively reinforce a behaviorist:

There was a hush as, high above us, he struck up the first great D minor chords of Bach's Chaconne. All at once, and with utter certainty, I had found my link with the center. The moonlit Altmühl Valley below would have been reason enough for a romantic transfiguration; but that was not it. The clear phrases of the Chaconne touched me like a cool wind, breaking through the mist and revealing the towering structures beyond. There had always been a path to the central order in the language of music, in philosophy and in religion, today no less than in Plato's day and in Bach's. That I now knew from my own experience.[2]

I had this passage in mind when I talked to Heisenberg in Munich after my visit with Weizsäcker and Gopi Krishna. When I asked him how it could be that science in his hands or Einstein's (a portrait of Einstein was on the wall over his left shoulder) could be so contemplative and in B. F. Skinner's hands so twisted out of shape as to become a weapon, he answered: "Scientists now work as stonemasons did once on cathedrals. They put the stones next to one another with great attention to detail and the work of the fellow next to them, but they have no sense of the architectonics of the whole. And sometimes they do not even have a sense of the purpose of a cathedral." His eyes under his great bushy eyebrows actually twinkled. He was too thin and bald to make a good Santa Claus, but decked out in the appropriate costume, the grandfatherly Heisenberg was one of those archetypal wise old men whom Yeats had been able to celebrate but not emulate:

> One asks for mournful melodies;
> Accomplished fingers begin to play.
> Their eyes mid many wrinkles, their eyes,
> Their ancient, glittering eyes, are gay.

As Heisenberg reflected over the climax of physical science in his lifetime, he agreed with his colleague, Weizsäcker, that the great age of natural science was nearing its end. In finishing his own Unified Field Theory, he felt that an era was over. When he was a young musician, Heisenberg had felt that the great era of European music had reached its consummation and that the mind of Europe could be better raised to new heights in physics. His intuition had always been good, and now he intuitively felt that our culture was reaching its limit. The ecological limit on the growth of civilization, he maintained, only expressed the outward sign of the limits to growth of the human spirit in the material dimensions it had been exploring since the Renaissance.

There was no sadness in Heisenberg's sense of the passing of the great age of natural science. He was a master surveying a satisfying life of full creation. He saw the limit and accepted it with humility.

Since Heisenberg felt that human culture could now reorient itself by making the limit part of its new bearings, I asked him if he felt that the direction Weizsäcker was taking into Eastern mysticism was a path others could take to move from an abusive technology to a more contemplative science. He answered that there was no question that the East had a knowledge we needed, that this knowledge was stronger than the West's feeble attempts to reduce consciousness to electronics and information theory, but he still felt that the new directions would appear in the West. He was a Western man; as a musician and a scientist, he was more a follower of Pythagoras than of Patanjali.

The work of Heisenberg and Weizsäcker should demonstrate that if there are "two cultures," they are not, as Lord Snow indicated, science and the humanities, but Archimedean and Pythagorean forms of knowledge. On the Archimedean side we have all the technological attempts, whether agricultural, industrial, or military, to alter and control nature; on the Pythagorean side we have all the cosmological thinkers for whom art, religion, and science are different idioms in a single language of contemplation. Within the Archimedean ranks are Bacon, Harvey, Lavoisier, Pasteur, Teller, and von Braun; within the Pythagorean ranks are Kepler, Descartes, Pascal, Newton, Faraday, Whitehead, Einstein, Schrödinger, Heisenberg, and Weizsäcker. There are two cultures, but the dividing line cuts at right angles across the boundary between science and the humanities; for if contemplative mysticism can appear in science, superstition and priestcraft can as well. Certainly the science of Skinner bears the same relation to the scientific tradition as the Inquisition does to Christianity.

Weizsäcker's interest in yoga, like Schrödinger's interest in Vedanta before him,[3] grew out of his own meditations on the psychological implications of the quantum theory. If subatomic particles are more mathematical *forms* than discrete pieces of *material,* and if the *modes* of perceiving these forms through laboratory instruments and mathematics alter the material itself, then, as Heisenberg would say, we no longer have a science of nature, but a science of the mind's knowledge about nature.[4] As Pythagoras said, "All is number." Although we have only a few phrases and many legends of Pythagoras, men as different in religious temperament as Whitehead and Russell are willing to accept his apotheosis. Whitehead's celebration in particular is worth recalling:

The field is now open for the introduction of some new doctrine of organism which may take the place of the materialism with which, since the seventeenth century, science has saddled philosophy. It must be remembered that the physicists' energy is obviously an abstraction. The concrete fact, which is the organism, must be a complete expression of the character of a real occurrence. Such a displacement of scientific materialism, if it ever takes place, cannot fail to have important consequences in every field of thought.

Finally, our last reflection must be, that we have in the end come back to a version of the doctrine of old Pythagoras, from whom mathematics, and mathematical physics, took their rise. He discovered the importance of dealing with abstractions; and in particular directed attention to number as characterizing the periodicities of notes of music. . . .

Truly, Pythagoras in founding European philosophy and European mathematics, endowed them with the luckiest of lucky guesses—or, was it a flash of divine genius, penetrating to the inmost nature of things?[5]

If mathematical form becomes more basic than matter itself, then it follows that science, the cultural process in which the mind develops *modes* for the knowing of *forms*, is an inseparable part of nature. The subjective-objective distinction collapses. It does little good, then, to talk confidently of "facts" when you do not understand the *structure* of consciousness through which one can entertain the *content* of facts.

The difficulty always arises when one confidently thinks in terms of a subjective "inside" world and an objective "outside" world. We are not standing outside nature and observing it through a window. We ourselves are a part of the nature we seek to describe, and through what Whitehead calls "the withness of the body" we can discover the correspondence between neurons and neutrinos.

The mechanists seek to reduce consciousness to electrochemical behavior; the mystics seek to show that "behavior" is an abstraction taken out of context. If there is a structure to consciousness (the way in which the brain processes information), and this can be expressed scientifically in mathematics; and if there is a structure to matter, and this can be scientifically expressed in the mathematics of the quantum theory, then the forms of one relate to the forms of the other through pure form, the structure of structures, the Logos. In other words, it is not the case that consciousness is created out of behavior; behavior is a construct built up out of consciousness. It is not "In the beginning was the flesh, and the flesh developed words," but "In the beginning was the Word and the Word was made flesh."

The way that Weizsäcker would express this is to point out that our consciousness of nature is a real event in the "history of nature." Unfortunately, we discover the force of consciousness most often in negative ways: we discover the nature of matter by taking it apart; we gain information about events through their vanishing. In terms of information theory, an increase in information generates an increase in entropy elsewhere in the system. The "feedback" of consciousness to nature is called culture; when culture reaches a certain point in the "negative feedback loop," it can destroy nature. We can see this effect in the earth's ecosystem, for our culture is changing the earth's atmosphere and weather. The point of maximum information, or maximum civilization, will correspond with entropy, and we will reach the end of history—which is precisely what the ecologists and the mystics have been prophesying. If the mind is, therefore, an energy state in which the increase of information is generating an increase in entropy in the surrounding system, then, for all practical purposes, the mind has to be looked upon as a very real event in the physical system.

According to the Second Law of Thermodynamics, all physical systems are moving toward maximum molecular chaos; according to evolution, some organic systems are moving toward maximum molecular organization. The evolution of man created an order on one level that generated disorder on lower levels in the plant and animal kingdoms. Now the cultural evolution of consciousness through science is generating disorder on the lower levels of human culture. Through genetic engineering, behavioral modification, and electronic stimulation of the brain, there is an increase in information which generates an increase in entropy in the cultural system. Traditions come apart as they are touched by the new kinds of science and technology that are beyond the control of their political and religious institutions. Paolo Soleri has characterized the evolutionary process as one of complexification and miniaturization, and this process seems to be holding true for culture. As our scientific knowledge has reached incredible levels of complexification, it has miniaturized itself into an increasingly smaller elite. Thus the growth of knowledge has a negative feedback loop not only to nature, but also to culture.

Now the yogis would claim that just as there is a negative feedback of consciousness to nature and culture, so, in terms of the laws of symmetry, is there a positive feedback. But before we can observe the positive feedback of consciousness to the body of the planet, we must first observe it in our own bodies. When a yogi stops his heart or alters other physical conditions hitherto thought to be part of the involuntary nervous system, he demonstrates that "matter" is subordinate to "mind." When a devout Christian develops the stigmata on Good Friday, he demonstrates the same priority of consciousness. Symbol is clearly dominant, for how is it that the devotee selects the right cells in the right symbolic spots, and does not miss and bleed from the cheek or forearm? When Swami Rama stopped his heart for seventeen seconds at the Menninger Institute under conditions of precise scientific observation, he closed a chapter of Western medicine and showed that the old Cartesian split between the *res extensa* and the *res cogitans* had been carried over into our medical textbooks in terms of the autonomic and voluntary nervous systems. This is only the first of many anomalies now being registered; as the anomalies accumulate, they will force the community of scientists to generate a new "paradigm" and Whitehead's prophesy will come true. The yogis insist that when the consciousness of mankind is raised to this new level, then matter will be spiritualized and the positive feedback to the body of the earth will be visible. Consciousness will then surround nature and culture to give us "a new heaven and a new earth." Of course, the Second Law will still remain to demand its price, and that is why many evolutionary thinkers feel that this transformation cannot be anything but apocalyptic.

Information is thus not simply a vague and less real copy or impression of a physical event. Information is just that, a form that works upon the probabilities of future events. If we speak of the laws of chance, we do not speak of the chance of laws. The freedom of chance is created by the very structure that underlies it; nothing is more limited and totally determining than absolute chaos. Consciousness is a moving form that evolves toward maximum organization and improbability, and it feeds upon the physical systems that move toward maximum molecular disorganization and probability. The difficulty between our notions of matter and of mind arises because science sees nature *diachronically*, and as such sees all systems as moving toward entropy—not because the universe is necessarily moving toward entropy, but because to see things *through* time means to choose to see things moving in that direction. When we build a cyclotron to search for elementary particles, we do not observe elementary particles; we observe what happens when we try to search for elementary particles. Mysticism observes the universe *synchronically;* it stops time, the very breath and heartbeat of the meditating observer's time, to open the still point of the turning world, and to see the universe at right angles to the flow of time. To explain this, consider music: the family dog listening with us to Bach on the phonograph hears the sounds, the successive pulses of noise through serial time; but he cannot perceive the fugue. He is perceiving sounds *diachronically*, and knows only their vanishing; when the music is gone, it is gone; we, however, are perceiving the sounds *synchronically* as music; when the music is finished, it is gathered up into resolved form; it is consummated in pure consciousness; the very vanishing of the music is the very condition that gives us aesthetic joy in the accumulation of the forms. Thus, as T. S. Eliot would say:

> To be conscious is not to be in time,
> But only in time [is] the moment in the rose-garden.

The yogi in samadhi is not in time. Quite literally, he has suspended his breath and the pulse of his heartbeat to step outside the time of his physical system to observe the consummation of all forms in the nadam, the music of the spheres. The physicist must come at the universe in the direction of time. As Weizsäcker explains it:

The structure of time is the basis of unity for physics. The structure must be conceptually analyzed by a logic of temporal propositions and a theory of probability as the form of an empirical prediction of the future. The use of the concept of probability in physics determines the structure of its two fundamental theories which are mutually related, quantum theory and thermodynamics. They are mutually related insofar as statistical thermodynamics presupposes an elementary theory and also because the concept of measurement in quantum theory cannot be explained apart from the thermodynamic concept of irreversibility. In a stage we have not yet reached these two theories therefore ought to merge into one. . . .

Quantum theory is a theory of probabilistic prediction of decisions about contingent alternatives (measurements). Up to any given time only a finite number of alternatives are capable of being decided (the finite factualness of the past), but the number of future alternatives still to be decided is unlimited (openness of the future). This results at any given time in a finite-dimensional quantum theoretical phase space which may be represented by the smallest physical objects (elementary particles) in a compact, expanding regular space.

This hypothetical approach is philosophically significant because it accounts for all of physics as a theory of prognosticating the probability of alternatives which can be empirically decided. Even without any further hypothetical considerations it is clear that this falls within the scope of quantum theory. This is often considered a kind of observer-related subjectivism. On the other hand, this kind of physics is doubtlessly intersubjective: different observers can only have experiences which are mutually compatible, unless they are in error. We cannot think of a single observer for whom the future is factual. This "objective subjectivity" is denoted by the concept of information. Deriving the qualities of "matter" from a count of decidable alternatives may be expected to reduce the concepts of mass, energy, and information *to a single unifying, fundamental principle of moving form* [my emphasis]. In this view, the physical world would be— approximating Kant—that which can appear to a finite mind. Insofar as finite mind or consciousness is capable of appearing to itself empirically, it would itself constitute "matter." I have on occasion expressed this in a formula which follows Schelling: "Nature is spirit which does not have the appearance of spirit."[6]

Nature is spirit which does not have the appearance of spirit for those perceiving it diachronically; for those perceiving it synchronically in the consciousness of samadhi, nature is once again spirit. Mass, energy, and consciousness are seen to be a single continuum and not a broken universe of real objective events and unreal subjective thoughts.

To consider these abstract notions in physical forms, let us go back to the Pythagorean fondness for triangles and construct a model, a *yantra,* to express the continuum of mass, energy, and consciousness.

Let us read the diagram from left to right, from I through IV, from the hot red into the cooler blue of the spectrum. Starting with the top of the left side, we begin with the hot red line of Chaos. Sense perceptions bombard the individual and register not as "facts" but as "events." As one thinks about these events and arranges them in patterns, both conscious and unconscious, he moves away from the hot red of immediate sensation to the warm orange line of "ideas." The four triangles springing from the red line move inward to another plane of order and reduce the complexity of perception to the tighter focus of plane II, Ideas. Ideas are *Gestalten,* forms, patterns; but one must articulate these forms with one another. So we move further inward, again tightening the focus, as now three triangles spring from the orange plane into the yellow plane of III, Theories. To think about ideas is to develop a theory, a hypothesis which, if tested by a return to the hot red plane of sense events, gives one a scientific model of experience. But, ironically, to gain theoretical information, one moves toward high levels of abstraction where the hot and immediate plane of events is left far behind. If one continues this process to develop a theory of theories, a structure of structures, a metalanguage, metamathematics, or metaphysics, then he moves further away from the plane of experience into the plane of pure abstraction. Here on the cool green plane of level IV, Logos, we encounter the paradox that there is an inverse relationship between sense experience and certainty: to the degree that one develops an advanced science of nature one leaves the sense experience of nature behind. The further we go into the yantra, the further we are into the cool shades of contemplation and the further we are from the hot immediacy of events. At the level of Logos, there is the knower and the known, the primary duality, for two green triangles spring from the yellow plane of III to point toward the fourth plane, the green plane of Logos. But the structure of structures reflects the known back into the knower, for the Logos is not simply the structure by which the brain processes information, it is the formula by which the nerves fire and the stars pulse; it is the intelligibility principle that orders all forms: stars, nerves, crystals. The form which underlies all forms points to something beyond form, beyond knower and known. As we contract physical consciousness to the vanishing point, knower and known dissolve into a single cosmic

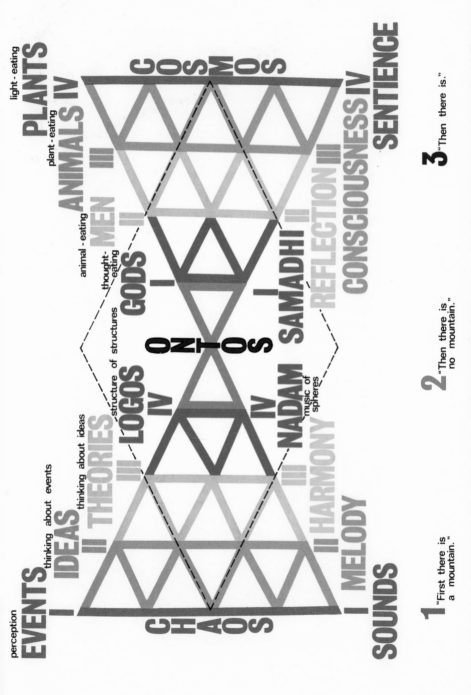

light - eating

PLANTS

plant - eating

ANIMALS IV

animal - eating

MEN III

thought - eating

GODS II

structure of structures

LOGOS IV

thinking about ideas

THEORIES III

thinking about events

IDEAS II

perception

EVENTS I

COS M OS

ON TO S

CHAOS

SENTIENCE

CONSCIOUSNESS IV

REFLECTION III

SAMADHI II

NADAM I

music of spheres

HARMONY III

MELODY II

SOUNDS I

1 "First there is a mountain."

2 "Then there is no mountain."

3 "Then there is."

consciousness, and the point expands to infinity in a new dimension. From the green plane of Logos there springs the single triangle that points to the Point, Ontos, pure Being. In the terms of Plotinus, this is the First Hypostasis, God the Father, Brahman beyond the created universe itself. In the yantra pure Being is the color of ultraviolet, the sacred purple, for as the hot red of sensation is blended with the cool blue of contemplation, the spiritual resolution is expressed as purple. It is not without reason that purple has always been revered as the spiritual color and that the amethyst was chosen for the stone of a bishop's ring.

When sensory consciousness in meditation begins to narrow, it discovers that there is another consciousness that widens in reciprocity with the other's narrowing. On the red plane of Chaos, the triangle of Ontos is a tiny invisible point, but by the time we reach the center in Ontos, the triangle is at its widest. Then God is visible. At the level of physical sensation and Chaos, God is not visible. God is to the universe what grammar is to a language; just as I cannot rip the grammar of English out of my mouth to prove to you that it exists, so I can't rip God out of the physical universe to show Him to you and prove that He exists.

If the progression from Events to Logos seems abstract, then we can consider the lower line of the triangle, which expresses the same set of relationships in terms of sound. Since the Hopis and the Hindus say that the universe is music, not matter, that all is energy and vibration, then sound is a primary expression of the levels of consciousness.

At the first level, the red plane, is physical sound. As we move inward, we come to patterned sound, to Melody. As melodies are articulated with one another, and the principles of counterpoint and harmony are developed, we approach the grammar of the language of sound, level III, Harmony. As we continue to move inward, we approach the music of music, the harmony of all harmonies, the metamusic that the Indians

call the Nadam and Kepler called the "Music of the Spheres."
This Nadam is the sound one listens to in meditation, the
orchestration of all sounds, of every electron in its orbit and
every planet in its orb.

Thus these levels of sound correspond to levels or planes
of consciousness. The dog hears sounds, the child hears melodies, the musician hears harmonies, and the mystic hears
the Nadam. These four planes of consciousness move in ascending order to the Point of Ontos; once we are in Ontos,
we can then move in a descending order of consciousness
back to the physical plane of sounds. In the yantra this is
expressed as going through the point from the left to the right
and moving out of the major triangle on the left into the
major triangle on the right. There we move from the pure
Being of Ontos to plane I (the blue line), Nirbikalpa
Samadhi. This is the highest state of mystical consciousness
for man, the state of being in which one is conscious of God
and man at the same time. This is the consciousness of the
gods. The second and lower state of Samadhi (expressed in
the green line) is Sabikalpa Samadhi. This is the consciousness of a yogi who must close his eyes and withdraw from
the world in meditation to see God. For an advanced yogi
in nirbikalpa samadhi, meditation is no longer the only
way to God; he continually sees God as the ground to any
figure that might be before him. When we come down from
the two stages of Samadhi to level II, Reflection, we come to
the intellectual plane of consciousness in which artist and
scientist do their work. The rational plane of being expresses
the present evolutionary level of man. As we move down to
the next level, III, we come to Consciousness; this is the level
of animals. Beyond that is level IV, Sentience, the level of ir-
ritability of plants.

If we look at the line on the top of the right major triangle,
we can see that these levels of consciousness in Creation can
be expressed in the chain of being of the Creatures. First there

are those plants that eat the light through photosynthesis; then there are those animals that eat the plants that eat the light; then there are those men who eat the animals that eat the plants that eat the light; and lastly there are those gods or devas who eat the thoughts of men who eat the animals that eat the plants that eat the light. In the words of the Upanishads:

Now if a man worships another deity, thinking the deity is one and he another, he does not know. He is like a beast for the Devas. For verily, as many beasts nourish a man, thus does every man nourish the Devas. If only one beast is taken away, it is not pleasant; how much more when many are taken! Therefore, it is not pleasant to the Devas that men should know this.[7]

The cosmic food-chain is an energy symbiosis, from the plants that feed off the sun to the devas and asuras that feed off the astral emanations of collective human thought. Just as we corral beasts to keep them in their place for our use, and as we sit on the fence and watch them ruminate all day long, we wonder how they can stand to eat all the time; so do the gods and demons corral us in history, and as they sit on the edge, they wonder how we can stand to *think* all day long. Within our corrals of history they come to stir up our wars and passions, so that we can be fat with the astral emanations that sustain them. Knowing that we are afraid of death, they catch us with its linked opposite, sexuality. Eros is thus the attractive jailkeeper in the prison of Thanatos.

As we step back from the yantra, we can see that the triangles are really pulsating, Yeatsian gyres. The rhythm is threefold: Chaos, Ontos, Cosmos. It is the sound of "AUM": "Ahhhh," the ecstasy of creation; "Oooooo," the ecstasy of maintenance; "Mmmmm," the ecstasy of destruction—Brahma the Creator, Vishnu the Preserver, and Shiva the Destroyer.

As sheer physical sensation is threaded through the point

of Ontos, it comes out as the spiritualized matter becoming a universe. Chaos is transformed and becomes Cosmos. This pulse is also the pulse of the yogic sadhana: first, physical sensation; then, the denial of physical sensation as we close our eyes in meditation; then, following experience of the higher states, comes the return to the world of the physical "to know it for the first time." This is one meaning of the Zen koan: "First there is a mountain, then there is no mountain, then there is." And this pulse is also the structure of Descartes's *Meditations.* First he withdraws from nature and calls all his perceptions and ideas into doubt. Then he realizes that even if he imagined the worst—that he was being deliberately deceived by a devil—he would still have to exist in order to be deceived. And then he asks himself how he knew that and he realizes it was through reason, through the system of contradictions. He strips away all content from thought to see the structure and knows that he must exist to be deceived. Having discovered the certainty of reason, freed of physical sensation, he then vows to return to nature to build up through the reason a whole new science of nature.

And now that I know Him I have the means of acquiring a perfect knowledge of an infinitude of things, not only of those which relate to God Himself and other intellectual matters, but also of those which pertain to corporeal nature in so far as it is the object of pure mathematics.[8]

And yet there is still more to be seen in the yantra, for yantras are nothing if not forms within forms. The yantra contains two invisible triangles and two visible triangles, thus giving us the form of the Jungian quaternity. If we examine the major triangle on the left, we see that it has at its base four orange triangles. But inside the quaternity of triangles is the trinity of three triangles; inside the trinity of triangles is the duality; but in the midst of duality, there is the One.

The whole major triangle on the right is composed of four pyramids, each containing four triangles, thus giving us the square (the quaternity again) of four, or sixteen. If I were a mathematician, I could probably see all sorts of numerical factors in this. But suffice it to say that the yantra is a Pythagorean celebration of the form of the triangle. Although this yantra came to me in contemplation, it should be obvious that this form is not a personally created diagram or model. It is an archetypal form and shows that the imagination as well as the dream can take us into the "collective unconscious."

If one takes this two-dimensional yantra and sees it as a three-dimensional Klein bottle or Möbius strip, he can see that the form curves back upon itself for the red of Chaos to touch the red of Cosmos. The intervening levels of consciousness are real events which make a cosmos much more than chaos, as the yantra explains. Thus this form becomes a model for contemplation, in Weizsäcker's words, "to reduce the concepts of mass, energy, and information to a single unifying fundamental principle."

Since all forms are by definition forms of consciousness, a moving form is the very essence of the consciousness of space-time. As Kant pointed out: we can conceive of objects without time, but we cannot conceive of time without objects. All time is, therefore, conscious time. Evolutionary time is an acceleration of consciousness in which we shift from moving through time, as if it were an invisible tunnel, to moving by means of time, as if it were a springboard. In cultural evolution there is a positive feedback upon the now consciously evolving organism to adjust the design of the cultural vehicle in which man moves through space-time.

We can better understand these abstractions about time if we think of sex. Amoebas are sexual and immortal; they do not reproduce themselves and die, they simply divide themselves *ad infinitum*. Man is sexually reproductive and mortal. In the ecstatic heightening of his consciousness of time in orgasm, he reproduces himself, and then feels unconsciously that he is on the other side of youth and that much closer to death: hence the Oedipal struggle between parent and child.

All mythologies are mythologies of love and death, Eros and Thanatos. If we go back as far as Lascaux, we see there on the walls of the cave the symmetrical pairing of male and female signs and animals and images of death.[9] The scene from the pit at Lascaux is the primordial icon, for there we see the beasts of the Great Mother and the dead, prostrate ithyphallic man. As we move forward from the hunting society of Lascaux to the agricultural society of Çatal Hüyük in 6500 B.C., we still see the same pairing of love and death. The dead were buried under the very beds upon which a new generation was conceived. And on the walls of the shrines, breasts were placed as sacred symbols, but in each nipple was placed a vulture's beak—inside the breast that gave life to the flesh was the vulture's beak that ripped the flesh from the corpse. These insights are millennia older than Freud, and, in many ways, Freud misunderstood the nature of iconography and symbolism. These icons are not symbols of sexuality; it is sexuality which is a symbol of time, human, tragic time.

Human time is much different from animal time, and, once again, it is human sexuality that expresses the difference. Animals go into heat and are open to sexuality only for a season, but man (like the dolphin) is open to sex at all times. Weizsäcker sees this as a very important point.

Here we can learn from evolutionist biology. Constant readiness for sexual intercourse is, biologically speaking, a peculiarity of the primates, if not of man alone. It is precisely not the "animal in man" which looks for constant sexual fulfillment.[10]

Because man is open to sexuality at all times, sexual attraction is at work at all times, and so these lines of force must be contained within a stronger field of culture. Hence the great emphasis upon sexual mores in all cultures. When chimpanzees are in heat, the female takes to the center of the camp and mates with young and old. But in man sexual attraction is extended through time and generates the form of time we call the family. Sexuality is not simply Brownian movement; it is a force that has direction, for it is at once the agent of natural selection and the basis for culture. The Indian word for this vector that is at once physical and psychic is "prana" and, as Weizsäcker observes:

The concept of Prana is not necessarily incompatible with our physics. Prana is spatially extended and vitalizing. Hence above all it is moving potency. The quantum theory designates something not entirely remote from this with the term "probability amplitude." The relationship may become clearer, when we consider the possibility as a strictly futuristic concept, that is, as the quantified expression of that towards which "the flow of time" is pressing to evolve.[11]

The flow of time in evolution thus holds the key to the relationship between mind and nature in the quantum theory, and the relationship between increasing molecular disorder in matter (probability states indicated by the Second Law) and increasing molecular organization in life (improbability states indicated by evolution). It is just this flow of time in evolution and human sexuality that is central to Gopi Krishna's attempt to demonstrate the biological basis for the psychological claims of yoga.

The writings of Gopi Krishna have a particular interest because he comes to yoga independent of the traditional guru-disciple system; he also comes to the authoring of scholarly books independent of a university education. By stepping to the side of Indian and Western systems of education, he has moved into an area of personal experience that now seems to be at the forefront of both Indian and Western culture.

In his autobiography,[12] Gopi Krishna describes how, after years of meditation, he released an energy that exploded in his body with immediately dangerous and harmful results. And yet it was the very physiological process of the transformation going wrong that helped him to see the whole physiological basis of the yogic transformation. Presumably, if Gopi Krishna had had a guru to watch over him and protect him, the process would have gone smoothly, with only a change from subtler to subtler states of consciousness in a body perfectly prepared. When, in Gopi Krishna's case, the psychic energy took a wrong turn into a wrong channel in the spinal column, his whole body burned with a painful energy that illuminated the "biological basis of religion and genius." And so we encounter a paradox: because Gopi Krishna was a yogic autodidact, he fell into errors that led to discoveries; because he was not widely read in yoga, he came at yoga through experience and not Sanskrit terms. Thus his autodidacticism is both his strength and his weakness; he is at once humble that he is not a scientist or scholar, and proud that he was able to do on his own what scientists and scholars have not done. Having accomplished much on his own, he has the strength of independence and the weakness of suspicion that other yogis are simply mouthing traditions and not expressing personal experience.

When Gopi Krishna was in trouble from the burning energy roaring through his spinal column, he tried to find a teacher to help him, but he could not. All seemed to know of yoga only through texts and word of mouth. In desperation he sent a wire to India's most famous saint and wise man, Sri Aurobindo. A while later he received the reply that, yes, indeed, he had raised kundalini to the seventh chakra by Tantric means and that he must seek out another Tantric yogi who had raised it to the seventh chakra in a similar manner. Gopi Krishna is a Tantric yogi, but Sri Aurobindo was not.

Tantric yogis work much more directly with the physiology of the body and the central nervous system than the more contemplative yogis of the Vedic system. The Tantrics maintain that there is enormous energy locked into sexuality, which, if released from the lower end of the spine, can flow up the spinal column to bring divine illumination to the brain. Along this spinal column, the Tantrics also claim, are spinning wheels (chakras) of psychic energy that govern the body's functions; these are said to be knots by which the soul is tied down to the body. At the base of the spine in the ordinary man this psychic energy is said to lie dormant; the mythological image given for this is a sleeping serpent whose mouth has closed over the opening to the inner spinal column that leads upward to the brain. The name of the serpent is "kundalini," and the process by which the serpent is awakened and led upward through the spinal column to the brain is called "Kundalini Yoga." As this energy moves upward, touching each chakra as it goes, it unties each knot until finally the soul is released from its bondage to the body and the now illuminated being achieves liberation. In the Christian tradition of the Book of Revelation, these chakras are called "the seven churches in Asia" or "the seven seals." "And when he had opened the seventh seal, there was silence in heaven about the space of half an hour."

Now because Sri Aurobindo did not serve Gopi Krishna as a Tantric guru, Gopi Krishna concluded that Aurobindo was merely a writer of books and that he alone of modern yogis had discovered what he calls in his latest book "The Secret of Yoga." But if one knows more about Aurobindo's Integral Yoga, one can see why he would not serve as a last-minute Tantric guru for a man who had felt he didn't need a guru in the first place. The difference between the

Tantric path and that of Aurobindo has been very clearly explained by Satprem.

Generally in the "normal" man these centres are asleep or closed or only allow the smallest little current necessary for his bare existence to filter through; he is really walled up in himself and communicates only indirectly with the outer world, within a very limited circle; in fact, he does not see other men or things, he sees himself in others, himself in things and everywhere; he cannot get out. With yoga the centres open. They can open in two ways, from bottom to top or from top to bottom, according to the methods practised: the traditional yogic and spiritual methods or the yoga of Sri Aurobindo. By the power of concentrations, exercises, one day we may feel an ascending Force which awakes at the base of the vertebral column and climbs from level to level right up to the top of the head with an undulating movement just like a serpent; at each level this Force *pierces* (violently enough) through the corresponding centre which opens and at the same time opens us to all universal vibrations or energies which correspond to the frequency of this particular centre. With the yoga of Sri Aurobindo the descending Force opens very slowly, gently, these very centres, from top to bottom. Often enough the lower centres do not open at all till much later. This process has an advantage if we understand that each centre corresponds to a *universal* mode of consciousness or energy; if, from the very beginning, we open the lower vital and subconscient centres, we risk being now swamped not by our own small personal affairs but by universal torrents of mud; we become automatically connected with the Confusion and the Mud of the world. This is why traditional yogas definitely required the presence of a Master who protects. With the descending Force this danger is avoided and we face the lower centres only after establishing our being solidly in the higher superconscient light. Once in possession of these centres, the seeker begins to know beings, things, the world and himself in their reality, as they are, for he no longer catches external signs, no longer doubtful words, gestures, all that immured dumb show, nor the veiled face of things, but the pure vibration in each thing, each being, at every stage, which nothing can camouflage.[13]

Because Tantra Yoga works from the bottom up, it is more rooted in the physiology of the body and much more directly concerned with sexuality. In the yoga of Aurobindo, one is counseled to move beyond sexuality into the psychic and overmental planes of consciousness. In the yoga of Gopi Krishna one has to be celibate only during the six-month period in which kundalini is rising. Because we Americans live in a culture that is saturated with sexual iconography, we are naturally more attracted to Tantra. "If one falls to the ground, he must use the ground to rise." In some forms of Tantra Yoga one has ritual intercourse with a female, a "shakti," and hopes that by stimulating sexuality, but holding back from orgasm, he will awaken kundalini. Since orgasm is the peak of time, the Tantric yogi hopes that by unlocking its mysteries he will release himself from the bonds of time. This nonorgasmic approach to sexuality is beginning to become part of the counterculture; it is finding artistic expression in many places, but with particular vividness in the writings of Doris Lessing.[14] The difficulty is that this mass approach to the esoteric techniques of Tantra is, as Satprem has pointed out, very dangerous.

In the ancient esoteric world there were two basic technologies of psychic energy: one was the astral-plane technology of death, the other of sexuality; the Aztecs were notorious for the former, and the Indians and Tibetans of the Left-Hand Path for the latter. Through public human sacrifice, the Aztec priests created a technology of terror; they would dramatically prolong the sacrifice to build up the astral emanations of the victim and the excited and terrified audience, and then in the climax of ripping out the heart and sending the flayed body thumping down the steps of the pyramid they would fuse the collective unconscious of the multitude into the forms of the priestly state. This is the technique of collectivization through terror that was rediscovered by Nazi Germany. But in the linkage of sexuality and death, orgasm as well as violent death can be turned into a technique for building up psychic emanations. In Tantric intercourse, or maithuna, the practitioners raise sexuality to the point of orgasm but never allow themselves to achieve it. As the psychic energy builds up, the unconscious opens, and kundalini can be awakened; but if the individuals are not Masters who can stare all cosmic sexuality and death in the face and blissfully raise the power to higher centers, then the whole collective subconscious engulfs them and they can go insane. A Master, of course, can confront the subconcious in safety, but American pop culture is not filled with Masters. The dangers arising from the popular interest in the Tantric technique of nonorgasmic genital coupling are considerable. Perhaps this is why even in the act of artistically describing this kind of sexuality the novelist Doris Lessing surrounds it with an atmosphere of unhealthiness and sadism. A much safer form of maithuna is the Tantric embrace or the joint meditation, where the fusing comes from the blending of auras and the subtler bodies, and where the etheric energy is exchanged through the heart chakra rather than the genital one.

Mass American culture is, of course, not ready for this etheric sexuality, and so its sexuality is hysterical and obsessive. In the iconography of *Deep Throat*, it is obsessed with the phallus, and in an hysterical attempt to overcome the split between mind and body by getting sexuality back into the head, it is trying to swallow the phallus whole. But as the profane always contains an exoteric mirror-image of a sacred, esoteric mystery, the obsessive images of American pornography reveal, like the temple statuary of Khajuraho, a hidden truth. Putting the semen into the head is what

Tantra Yoga is all about, and in his writing Gopi Krishna is very specific about how, when the kundalini is awakened through meditation, the prana of the semen is reversed and begins to flow up through the spinal column into the brain. As the sexual secretions go up the spinal column, an intense and ecstatic consciousness is generated, and the individual feels that he is both male and female at once, for the spinal column becomes a vagina and the brain becomes the womb for the birth of a divine child. The transformed yogi thus becomes an angelic androgyne. Interestingly enough, just this kind of imagery is rampant in the esoteric literature of India and the Near East.

If the individual becomes both a man and a woman, then he is no longer asexual like the timeless amoeba, or tragically mortal like the sexual human; he-she becomes eternal like a divine being. The Fall is reversed, for the time light bodies took to fall becomes the time falling bodies take to light. Once again, sexuality becomes a symbol of time.

This mystery of the reversal of the semen from the outside world to the inner one is found not only in yogic literature but in Gnostic writings as well. "The Jordan was caused by Jesus to flow upstream; it is the rising flood and this, as already mentioned, is the begetter of gods."[15] In other instances this process is associated with the imagery of the distillation of liquor; in the transformation of a coarse seed or grain into a subtly refined and clear liquid which passes through narrow spinal-like tubes, we have an image of the clear "spirits" which when taken into the brain produce an altered state of consciousness. In alcohol as with genital sexuality, we have an exoteric image of an esoteric truth. But the difficulty with the exoteric image is that it is reversed; it is, therefore, a lie, and to function effectively any lie must contain, but not express, the truth. In the contemporary counterculture we do not see the divine androgyne but the demonic hermaphrodite,[16] we see Alice Cooper or Mick Jagger rather than Sri

Aurobindo or Gopi Krishna. In that classic of the counter-culture, *The Politics of Experience*, R. D. Laing quotes the old Gnostic Gospel of St. Thomas that "the male and female must become one," and this is popularly interpreted to be an endorsement of bisexuality and gay liberation. But according to yoga these youth cultists are doing exactly the opposite of what the Gnostic Gospel intends; the semen taken into the head in this demonic fashion absolutely guarantees that the divine transformation cannot take place, for kundalini cannot rise to the brain. The lies of sex cults and drug culture deceive people because they refract but do not reflect the truth.

As Gopi Krishna sees it, sexuality has two functions: the first is the reproduction of the race as it now is; the second is the transformation of the race for the future. In the first kind of sexuality man's prana is expended outward in orgasm; in the second the prana is stimulated by focused consciousness in meditation and then drawn upward into the brain through the spinal canal. In this transformation, Gopi Krishna insists that the sexual secretions are changed and then physically carried up into the brain in a way that could be verified in the medical laboratory.

If the sexual basis of Tantra Yoga can be proven scientifically, as now "The Physiological Effects of Meditation" are beginning to be,[17] then the sexual nature of our culture will begin to shift. But perhaps it already has. The mechanists are claiming that they soon will be able to design a new man through genetic engineering; if so, then sexuality as a means of natural selection is obsolete. The culture of Eros and Thanatos will be at an end, which is perhaps one good reason that these same biologists speak of cloning and biological immortality in the same breath in which they speak of the end of sexual reproduction. But the mystics also are proclaiming the appearance of a new superman and the elimination of sexuality in reproduction.[18] If men are not driven by sex, but instead drive it upward toward their own transformation, then psychic culture will replace sexual culture, and new traits will be evolutionarily selected. This new psychic culture would be similar to the old educational culture. Because of university coeducation in America, individuals were presented with a choice of spouses, all with a uniformly higher level of intelligence than could be presented in a normal small town. When these educated people created their own small towns like Los Alamos, the process of selection produced very high levels of intelligence among the children. In fact, the IQ level of the students of Los Alamos High School is nothing short of phenomenal. As coeducation tended to make a wife into more than a decorative breeder of children with a good family background, so now will the new psychic sexuality encourage conscious conception through joint meditation-maithuna by two exaltedly conscious individuals. Gopi Krishna insists that if even one of the parents has gone through the kundalini transformation, then the child born to that couple will be extraordinary. With these children, Gopi Krishna sees the arrival of a new human race.

Most students of yoga who feel new energies flowing through them immediately set up shop as gurus and start taking on disciples, but Gopi Krishna will have none of this. The merchandising techniques of the Maharishi are abhorrent to him, and he regards Transcendental Meditation as little more than self-hypnosis[19]—which is strange since he respects and appeals to science, and Transcendental Meditation is one of the few yogic movements with a growing literature of scientific papers behind it. He will have nothing to do with modern, pop-culture forms of yoga showmanship with its theater of incense, flowers, red carpets, baubles, bangles, and beads. Among yogis, Gopi Krishna is something of a skeptical and down-to-earth Protestant. He is very suspicious of miracles, and the legendary abilities of a Sai Baba to materialize objects out of thin air would be scoffed at by him. This man of the colder northern climate of Kashmir has a practical air about him, and he looks down upon the exotic and luxuriant extravagances of the Indian subcontinent with a smile and a shake of the head. Gopi Krishna is a householder and a practical man; his interests are restricted to the physiological interface between Eastern yoga and Western science. Out of this interest has come his friendship with Professor von Weizsäcker.

If the physicist and the yogi do create a new field of knowledge in the Research Foundation for Eastern Wisdom and Western Science, the cultural implications will be enormous. And it is precisely these cultural implications that Gopi Krishna has in mind. Out of these new forms of knowledge will come new forms of education, and, after that, new elites. These elites will be scientists and scholars who not only have worked for their Ph.D.s in traditional universities, but have also spent the time in meditation to experience the elevation of kundalini. With the appearance of these new elites, the evolution of the human race will have reached its take-off speed. From Gopi Krishna's point of view our speed has already reached the dangerous point where we must either take off or crash.

In my humble view there is nothing that can counteract the overhanging threat of nuclear holocaust like the knowledge of Kundalini. Once the possibility of a spiritual rebirth with the arousal of this mighty power is accepted by mankind, Kundalini Yoga will provide the most sublime enterprise for the pure minded and intelligent adventurers of the age. To the share of this lofty class of men, adorned with the knowledge of the inner and the outer worlds, will fall the herculean task of educating humanity in the essentials of this almighty spiritual Law to guide the race to the glorious estate ordained for it.[20]

Although the political implications of this have not been thought out by the Eastern pandit, they are apparent to any Western pundit. Whether we are driving in the lanes of science or mysticism, we seem to have come to the end of the road for the liberal humanism that began in the Renaissance. The behaviorists want to eliminate freedom and dignity to achieve the behaviorally controlled state; the Club of Rome wants "a fundamental revision of human behavior . . . and the entire fabric of present-day society"; and the mystics want a "lofty class of men" who will keep watch over the flock of the human race. The elitist strain in Gopi Krishna's thought is slightly unsettling, for as he writes about heredi-tary predispositions leading toward a sensible social order, one has visions of a reinstitution of the caste system. Because Freiherr von Weizsäcker is a German aristocrat and Gopi Krishna is a Brahman, the union of their sensibilities seems doubly aristocratic. As an apostate Catholic I could sense immediately the possibilities for a new Papacy and a new College of Kundalini Cardinals.

When I questioned Gopi Krishna about this elitism, he replied: "Don't you think there is an elite ruling now? What you call democracy is the rule of the rich, the powerful, the highly educated, the rule of the few." Gopi Krishna wishes to change the elite from a material to a spiritual one. And if one takes *The Limits to Growth* seriously, then the ecologi-cal system of the planet can no longer support a culture in which a generation is raised with the expectation of earning the amount of money necessary to support a life of high consumption. The value system of mankind must change, and since kundalini cannot be elevated at the demands of the Total State, the value system must be changed through a natural religious transformation of man's world view. And this is precisely what Gopi Krishna is working for. Nevertheless, one cannot help but feel that Gopi Krishna has not really given the politics of mysticism much thought. Perhaps because he began his career as a political revolutionary, or perhaps because as a Cambridge graduate in classics he was more familiar with the *enantidromias* of history, Sri Aurobindo is a more intellectually satisfying writer on the roles of democracy and socialism in the future of civilization. While praising socialism, he is still quick to check its drive toward collectivism:

. . . there is this deeper truth which individualism has discovered, that the individual is not merely a social unit; his existence, his right and claim to live and grow are not founded solely on his social work and function. He is not merely a member of a human pack, hive, or ant-hill; he is something in himself, a soul, a being, who has to fulfill his own individual truth and law as well as his natural or his assigned part in the truth and law of the collective existence. He demands freedom, space, initiative for his soul, for his nature, for that puissant and tremendous thing which society so much distrusts and has labored in the past either to suppress altogether or to relegate to the purely spiritual field, an individual thought, will and conscience. If he is to merge these eventually, it cannot be into the dominating thought, will and conscience of others, but into something beyond into which he and all must be both allowed and helped freely to grow. That is an idea, a truth which, intellectually recognized and given its full exterior and superficial significance by Europe, agrees at its root with the profoundest and highest spiritual conceptions of Asia and has a large part to play in the moulding of the future.[21]

The best way to protect spirituality from religion is to have a secular counterforce to the sacred. One can select the priests of Israel, but no one can select her prophets; they come not out of civilization but out of the wildness of the desert. Not only is the sacred protected by the secular, but often its very energies of resacralization spring from the dirt of the profane. The masses of Palestrina and Lassus sprang from street songs, much to the shock of the hierophants of the day; and today new tellings of the Passion, like *Godspell*, are springing from hip culture and rock music. This relationship between the sacred and the secular seems to have been recognized by the American Founding Fathers. As Masons, they were religious men; but in working to prevent the establishment of a state religion, they affirmed that an open and secular culture of law was the best medium for the growth of human spirituality. Denmark has a state religion and all its ministers are salaried by the government; but no one comparing the religious imaginations of Denmark and America could deny that the difference between the two countries is the difference between a potted plant and a forest.

But there is one advantage that a religion has over science as an elite system. In religion the top and the bottom of society can think the same thought, though not in the same way. A peasant crucifix alongside a road and the Isenheim altarpiece by Grünewald are much closer together than a peasant counting sheep and a scientist doing quantum electrodynamics. When science approaches the point at which mankind can participate in it, it passes over into mythology, and there converges with religion and art. One cannot create a mythology with scientific methods, but one certainly can create science out of mythology, as Pythagoras, Plato, Newton, Marx, Freud, Jung, and Einstein show. In a mythological vision of the universe both folk art and high culture can achieve levels of excellence.

But Gopi Krishna is interested not so much in remythologizing science with yoga as in demythologizing yoga with science. He looks to a new "lofty class" of scientists with elevated kundalinis to take over the leadership of the world in the wake of a nuclear war. Lesser men may be corrupted by power, but Gopi Krishna feels confident that there can be no problems with men whose brains have been illuminated by kundalini. The new Catholic Church will not be like the old one. In his vision of nuclear war and the rise of a new scientific elite, Gopi Krishna's vision is indistinguishable from that of H. G. Wells, but in his case it is literally a vision for he has seen the images of planetary destruction while in a higher state of consciousness.

Weizsäcker, too, has feelings about the inevitability of nuclear war, and if his experiences in the last war had not checked his fantasies, he, too, might dream of an invisible international Pythagorean Brotherhood of Scientists and divinely illuminated men keeping weapons out of the hands of the children of the race.

"The fact that we physicists formed one family was not enough," Weizsäcker remarked after the war. "Perhaps we ought to have been an international Order with disciplinary power over its members. But is such a thing really at all practicable in view of the nature of modern science?"[22]

It is not. Such a priestcraft of science would use its disciplinary powers to preserve tradition against innovation, and another Galileo would be brought to his knees, another Bruno brought to the stake. But where does that leave us? Whether we choose the Archimedean State or the Pythagorean Brotherhood, our choices seem to be limited by the fact that we no longer have the time to avoid the choice. History reclaims us with each heartbeat, and if we try to run, the gods laugh to see man running out of time.

SIX

Planetary Mythologies

Analogy One

Imagine insects with a life span of two weeks, and then imagine further that they are trying to build up a science about the nature of time and history. Clearly, they cannot build a model on the basis of a few days in summer. So let us endow them with a language and a culture through which they can pass on their knowledge to future generations. Summer passes, then autumn; finally it is winter. The winter insects are a whole new breed, and they perfect a new and revolutionary science on the basis of the "hard facts" of their perceptions of snow. As for the myths and legends of summer: certainly the intelligent insects are not going to believe the superstitions of their primitive ancestors.

Analogy Two

Imagine a vehicle as large as a planet that began a voyage an aeon ago. After generations of voyaging, the mechanics lose all sense of who they are and where they are going. They begin to grow unhappy with their condition and say that the notion that they are on a journey in an enormous vehicle is a myth put forth by the ruling class to disguise its oppression of the mechanical class. There is a revolution and the captain is killed. Elated by their triumph, the mechanics proclaim the dictatorship of the proletariat and destroy the captain's log, which contains, they claim, nothing but the lies of the old ruling class.

Analogy Three

Imagine that you have just discovered a civilization as small as a DNA molecule. You want to establish contact, but since your dimensions prevent you from entering the same space-time envelope, you must search for other means of communication. From observing the civilization closely, you find that there is an informational class that seems to carry messages back and forth among parts of the society, and you observe further that these messengers are actually enzymes of a structure that is isomorphic to one of your own patterns of information. Since you cannot talk directly *to* the members of the civilization, you decide to talk *through* a patterning of the bits of information the enzymes carry back and forth. Unfortunately, the very act of trying to pattern an enzyme alters its structure so that a part of your own message is always shifted. It seems that the only time the enzymes are able to carry a high proportion of your own message is when their civilizational structure is either breaking apart or just about to come together again. Fascinated by the problem, you choose your opening and closing epochs carefully and begin to carry on an extended conversation with the civilization.

Each of these analogies indicates that information is subject to alteration and decay through time. Although I have chosen the idiom of science fiction, an understanding of this process of decay is not limited to modern times, for it was clearly understood by the ancient Egyptian sources of Vico's theory of history.

Two great remnants of Egyptian antiquity have come down to us. One of them is that the Egyptians reduced all preceding world time to three ages; namely, the age of gods, the age of heroes, and the age of men. The other is that during these three ages three languages had been spoken, corresponding in order to the three aforesaid ages; namely, the hieroglyphic or sacred language, the symbolic or figurative (which is the heroic) language, and the epistolary or vulgar language of men employing conventional signs for communicating the common needs of their life.[1]

An epoch begins with a divine consciousness of cosmic myth in the age of the gods. By the time of the following age of heroes half the cosmic myth is gone, and, with it, half the divine consciousness. By the time of the age of men the myth and the consciousness halve again, leaving only a quarter of the original. Finally, in the ultimate age of barbarism and chaos, little of the original myth or divine consciousness remains at all. But as entropy reaches its limit in chaos, there is a reversal in the cycle, a cosmic form is generated out of the only ground large enough for it, namely, chaos. Chaos creates the fertile decay in which the seeds left over from the previous age of gods spring to life to create a new cosmic myth and a new age of gods. We spiral back to the past in a future on a higher plane.

As an illustration of this historical process, consider the Sumerian civilization. The first age was definitely the age of the gods; men insisted that they did not build the great cities, that gods from the sky built them and brought to man all the arts of civilization.[2] As the colony began to grow and prosper, the gods departed, leaving only a steward, an *ensi*, to look after things in their absence. The gods said they would return, but given the relativistic time-shift, what may be only a short journey for them could take thousands of years of our historical time. But the memory of man is short; soon the *ensis* began to exercise power on their own terms, and stewardship evolved into kingship. For a while the kings ruled with respect for the old cosmic mythology, but with faction replacing faction, it was only a matter of a few centuries before the skepticism of the rulers was shared by the whole populace. As secularism and the philosophy of naked power grew, the cosmic myths that held the civilization together and rooted it in the universe were torn apart. Men no longer believed in anything. Since the society no longer held together on its own, it was compressed by force and militaristic terror. The military state, whether of Sargon of Agade or Moctezuma of Mexico, is the last desperate collectivization of a disintegrating society. But states organized for conquest inevitably organize their enemies to conquer them. In the ultimate age of barbarism and chaos, God tells Abraham to leave Ur and go "unto a land that I will show thee." Abraham leaves the sophisticated urbanism of Ur behind him to move back into a primitiveness that is on a higher moral level. And he leaves Ur just in time; the Elamite barbarians from the north invade and mighty Ur is given over to the wind. Thus the three ages of Sumerian civilization can be summarized in the following beliefs of the rulers: (1) "The gods rule through me"; (2) "I rule for the gods"; and (3) *"I rule!"*

It is easy to see the structure of Sumerian civilization because it is over and we are far enough away to observe its general form. But it is harder to perceive the form of our own immediate historical condition. Cultural transformations are so large that they are invisible to normal individuals. If you went around in England in the 1790's asking how it felt to be living in an age of industrial revolution, most people would not know what you were talking about. But if you went to see "the lunatic" William Blake, he would tell you about the meaning of the great transformation by moving back and forth from one end of history to the other in a notation especially designed for ideas that large— mythology. Marxists are not inclined to celebrate the virtues of mythopoeic thinking, but even the distinguished Marxist historian Eric Hobsbawm grudgingly recognizes its power:

It is never wise to neglect the heart's reasons which the reason knows nothing of. As thinkers within the terms of reference laid down by the economists and physicists, the poets were outclassed, but they saw not only more deeply but also sometimes more clearly. Few men saw the social earthquake caused by machine and factory earlier than William Blake in the 1790's who had yet little except a few London steam-mills and brick-kilns to go by.[3]

Events that are too large to be perceived in immediate history register in the unconscious in the collective form of myth, and since artists and visionaries possess strongly mythopoeic imaginations, they can express in the microcosm of their works what is going on in the macrocosm of mankind. Because they lack economic power, they are open to other possibilities, and they can cultivate other faculties. Ironically, it is only the man who is free to do without technology who is in a position to master it.

In the 1760's the visionary mechanists and the romantics were thinking in new modes that were to become part of the cultural transformation of mankind. Although Marx would insist that it is not the consciousness of men that determines their material condition, but their material condition that determines their consciousness, even he was willing to admit that the imagination could outrace economic development to elaborate an ideology in advance of its social need. For Marx the seventeenth-century Levelers were prophets of a future revolutionary Europe.

The Scottish Primitivists are another example of men developing an ideology in advance of its social need.[4] In 1770 they elaborated a theory, contrary to the Biblical account, that men evolved from wood-men to land-dwellers to settled city-dwellers. This vision of progress was quite different from the Christian's tragic vision of the Fall, so much so that Vico, in elaborating a similar theory a generation before, had been careful to explain that men fell into savagery as a result of the universal deluge. Contrary as the religion of progress was to the settled Christian vision of things, it became, nevertheless, the ruling ideology of industrial England by the time of the Great Exhibition of 1851.

Imaginative artists like Blake could understand the collective condition of society because the imagination is the opening to what Jung called "the collective unconscious." Precisely because this unconscious is collective, people can think the same thought at the same time even though they are separated by ordinary space. No one blew a whistle in Europe and said: "Stop thinking neoclassically; start thinking romantically in terms of primitives and nature." And yet the whole age did shift dramatically. Because we do not understand this process, we either ignore it or use terms like "spirit of the age." Hegel would call it the *Zeitgeist*, but whatever term is used, the radical implication is that human consciousness is not contained by the skull.

In our physical sciences we have long since gone beyond the eighteenth-century notion of dead hunks of matter moving in the black void of space. Yet our psychological sciences are still restricted to eighteenth-century mechanistic notions: minds are simply located hunks of gray matter moving in the black void of time. Once physicists tried to explain the phenomenon of the superconductor in terms of the incremental behavior of each electron; repeated failure finally convinced them that the electrons were not an aggregate society, but a single gas, a de Broglie wave.[5] In the superconducting society of electrons, when one electron is obstructed in the lattice, the others rush to pick it up and carry it in their path.

Perhaps the superconductor can provide us with a more contemporary model of culture and human consciousness. Cosmically, mankind is a single de Broglie wave, or what Christians would call the Mystical Body of Christ. Behavioral psychologists, bringing up the rear with their dead mechanistic physics, would assert that culture operates only through social interactions; for them space separates, and what does not touch physically or symbolically can have no effect. But the concept of space the behavioral psychologists take for granted has long since disappeared from physics. Even in nonrelativistic frames of reference, physicists assert that all is energy and vibration and that the solar wind reaches to the limits of the solar system. When sun, moon, and earth line up in an eclipse, magnetic perturbations give us earthquakes. All of which sounds as if we have spiraled back on a higher level of order to the astronomy of Stonehenge circa 1750 B.C. If we can spiral back astronomically to the archaic world view, we can also spiral back psychologically to realize that the mind of man is a collective and interpenetrating field.

The unconscious is not personal, but in order not to be swamped by infinite information, the brain functions as what Aldous Huxley called "a reducing valve." It shuts out the universe so that the individual can do what is in front of him. The million signals a second must be reduced to the few a second of the conscious mind. But the intuition and the imagination maintain an opening to the unconscious, which contains all the information that could not register in immediate consciousness. Since the immediate consciousness must work in a step-by-step incremental sequence of events, its perception of time is linear. Clearly, all the information cannot be restricted to that line, and so the time of the unconscious is out of time; the line must be widened and lengthened until it becomes a sphere if one is to achieve cosmic consciousness. In the space-time of the unconscious, the past and the future mysteriously interpenetrate in exactly the way the ancient Maya understood in their fantastic calendar of millions of years of cyclical, spiraling time.

Analogy Two is simply a version of the history of ancient Mexico. The priestly hierarchy knew that this planet earth was an enormous vehicle moving through infinite expanses of space and time. In the temples the priests kept the records of who we were, where we came from, and where we were going. But as the cosmic myth of the age of gods decayed through time, the distance between the decadent priesthood and the oppressed peasantry increased. The peasants rose up, attacked the ceremonial centers, and then abandoned them—to lower their horizons from the stars to their fields of growing corn.

Because ancient Mexico is not part of our historical awareness, visionaries have to speak to us in a different mythology if they are to recover man's lost cosmic orientation. Blake made one attempt, Yeats another. But mythological ideas are not always expressed with the genius of a Blake or a Yeats. An idea in the collective unconscious is what Lévi-Strauss would call a structure, but when that structure is performed in an individual's consciousness, it takes on the limitations of the personal content. The mythical message from the collective unconscious must travel through the distorting medium of culture and of the individual personality before it reaches the receiver. A mixture of the myth and the noise from the distorting medium is what reaches the receiver; so in order to be certain that he has the message right, the listener has to hear several different versions until he grasps the structure.[6] In the case of some occultists who transmit mythical information, there is as much noise as anything else.

In the old art of civilization the artist tried to achieve pure information and no noise in the clarity of a line of melody or poetry, but now in the days of "planetization," when the unconscious is flooding the culture, the new art is, of necessity, *about* the relationships in the scale: noise→information→music. In the old art there was only the one direction from noise to music, but in the new art there is a sliding scale of consciousness that moves back and forth through these values. This is most evident in the work of Stockhausen, and Stockhausen, especially in *Stimmung*, has gone beyond presenting descriptions of our age of chaos to create forms of our consciousness in the now emerging new age of the gods. But perhaps a better backdrop for our discussion of the unconscious is his *Hymnen*, for it sounds like a recording of the collective unconscious of the human race monitored aboard a flying saucer.

If one wishes to get a sense of the range between noise and information in contemporary planetary mythology, it is instructive to compare three quite different works. If we take Erich von Däniken's *Chariots of the Gods?*,[7] the occult *Urantia Book*,[8] and Doris Lessing's novel *Briefing for a Descent into Hell*,[9] we can see that often we reject ideas, not because the deep *structure* is unacceptable, but because the artistic *texture* of the work grates against our sensibilities. Out of the union of a vibrating body and a receiver comes a noise that is both in the work and in us.

Art is a *tone* of voice; it is personal and expresses the ego's relationship to the unconscious. The weakness and the greatness of art come from precisely this finiteness, this limitation. Mystics and mediums are often bad artists because they are too impersonal. Without yet having achieved the cosmic impersonality of myth, their art is all unconscious, and more dream than work of art, cliché as much as archetype. The artist has an enormous ego, and that is at once the substance of his art and the weight of his affliction; one has only to recall Wagner in this context. Afflicted as the artist may be with his ego, there is no question that his finitude is what really *matters;* the verses of a poetizing saint like Aurobindo or Yogananda cannot touch the heights of the poetry of a Milton or a Yeats.

It is precisely the tone of von Däniken that makes his *Chariots of the Gods?* so irritating. An autodidact who makes fun of the scientists and then tries to impress you with how scientific he is, von Däniken is continually posturing and looking over his shoulder to see if he has collected a following. Because von Däniken has had no professional training, his mind is open to all ideas, but it is so open that it is positively free-form. His *idée fixe* is that our religions and legends of God are cargo cults that sprang up ages ago when an astronaut from another planet happened to stumble on this primitive earth. Since then the story of the encounter has grown, legend by elaborating legend, until a whole coral island has risen to support the lives of countless priesthoods. The idea has all the materials for comedy, but, unfortunately, von Däniken is not up to making the fun out of it that Kurt Vonnegut does in his similar version of history, *The Sirens of Titan.* Von Däniken is very serious in challenging the experts who ridicule him, and so he has gone around the world having himself photographed, tape measure in hand, in front of the colossi of prehistory.

When you know what you are looking for, it is certainly not hard to find it. Von Däniken wants to find holes blasted out by rockets, so he takes the round wells of the Maya, the *cenote* at Chichén Itzá, and says that the limestone well is the result of a rocket blast. Curiously enough, he is willing to take the huge monolithic platform of the temple of Baalbek in Lebanon, which has no holes scoured out by rockets, and say that this, too, was a launching pad for rockets. Next he goes to the plain at Nazca in Peru to say that the long lines that can be seen only from the air are landing strips for the ships from space. The image of a World War II prop job chug-chugging in from Andromeda and needing a landing strip a few miles long is hilarious, but von Däniken is not sensitive to the perils of what Whitehead called "misplaced concreteness."

Von Däniken is nothing if not a literalist and a materialist. Gods are astronauts who need equipment to move around in; a halo about the head of a figure carved on the rock at Tasili N'ajjer is not the archetypal aura, but a space helmet. For von Däniken there is nothing complicated in the universe; all can be explained in terms of our present technology and three ordinary dimensions. For the lovers of materialism, either the von Däniken or the Soviet Zaitsev hypothesis of extraterrestrial intervention in prehistory is a way to be comfortable in an infinite universe. What pretends to be a bold and imaginative approach to space is, therefore, really one of the most literal, fundamentalist closures of the imagination possible. And yet the archaeological anomalies that von Däniken settles on, from Stonehenge to Easter Island, are real anomalies; and the quotations about spaceships in the old mythologies of the East, Near and Far, are there to give us pause. If von Däniken is an informational cell that the extraterrestrials are using to make their presence known, they have coded their cosmic message for a particular audience of very dense materialists.

If you are a god from outer space and you are trying to run the earth by press leak, then a different way to force the mechanists and engineers to lift their horizons a bit is to address yourself to the civil servant with his love of order, rationality, and common sense. *The Urantia Book*, like the *Pentagon Papers*, is just the kind of thing you would want to let fall into mankind's hands. Here is nothing less than a two-thousand-page archangel's operating manual and history of earth, otherwise known as Urantia at galactic headquarters. Everything is there, from the overseers' reports on our early programmed evolution, to position papers on the Lucifer Rebellion, to committee reports on our religions, institutions, and sexual customs. These reports are signed by "A Life Carrier and member of the original Urantia Corps and now a resident observer" or "Chief of the Seraphim stationed on Urantia." Parts of the book read like the cosmology expressed in C. S. Lewis's theological science fiction trilogy, but there are just enough differences in the account of Jesus's mission to be puzzling. The occult stories of Jesus's life claim that the Christ was a supremely highly evolved being from beyond our solar system who entered Jesus's body at the time of the baptism by John.[10] The mission of the Hebrew prophets was to prepare a human body with a high enough vibratory rate to make contact with the higher realms. The occultists claim that Jesus was the reincarnation of Elisha and that John the Baptist was the reincarnation of Elijah. About three different sources seem to go along with this version; however, *The Urantia Book* has a slightly different one, in which there is affinity between Jesus and Elisha, but not an actual reincarnation.

Now the really puzzling and interesting problem in terms of information and noise in the occult is why the many versions are so alike and yet so different. It almost seems as if there is, if one could discover it, a law waiting to be articulated in terms of semantic shift, something in the manner of Grimm's Law of consonantal shift. Then again, perhaps we are being too human, linear, and simple-minded to assume that there is one message that is the Truth and that the variations all come from the pickup of noise from the distorting and communicating medium. What if at the higher levels of meaning consciousness is like a hyperspace in which each point is equidistant from the other and where "the center is everywhere and the circumference is nowhere"? The mythologies of the occult seem to be like baroque music: there is an overall similar quality of sound and movement, but, upon examination, each piece of music is unique; Vivaldi and Scarlatti are similar and different. If we think of it in this way, we can see that art is a closer approximation of reality than science, and that information theory is incapable of dealing with the infinite variables and multiple meanings of poetry. Computer scientists and linguistic philosophers have an instinctive distaste for the ambiguity that makes their lives difficult. They continually try to translate life into a notation that is clear, precise, and capable of a single meaning for all observers. It is obvious that God is intelligent enough to be bored by such an automatic and repetitive universe, for He has designed one with a much more fascinating set of relationships between the unique and the universal. More fascinating and more poetic, for if one thinks in terms of, say, romantic poetry, he can see that there is not One Message that is romanticism; rather there are Wordsworth and Coleridge, Shelley and Keats.

The relationship between information and noise is thus a rich and complex one; it is at once symbiotic, like life and death, and relativistic, like time and space. For the hippie in the country the dandelion is a flower and a beneficent herb; for his father in the suburbs it is a cancerous growth that he must root out with force. But let us assume that we can sift the noise from the information, and let us further assume that there are gods and that they are trying to communicate with us in the fashion of Analogy Three. The informational cells are those persons who are open to pick up and carry the new information, but since each medium is a distorting medium, there is an inevitable addition of personal noise. If a person is open to a new world view, it can often mean that he is not firmly rooted in the reality of the old world view; as a lunatic or an alienated artist, his own neurotic traits can become magnified as they tremble with the new energy pouring in from the universal source. In the history of ideas a new idea is often first picked up by a crazy person, then elaborated by an artist who is more interested in its imaginative possibilities than in its literal truth; then it is picked up by a scholar or scientist who has become familiar with the idea through the work of the artist; the savant makes the hitherto crazy idea perfectly acceptable to the multitude, until finally the idea rests as a certainty in the hands of a bureaucracy of pedants. As Thomas Huxley said: "It is the customary fate of new truths to begin as heresies and to end as superstitions." If we look at the history of the idea of evolution, we see this process at work. First the eccentric lunatic Lord Monboddo claimed that we were all descended from monkeys and that it was only a crafty conspiracy of plucky midwives who cut off all the tails at birth that hid this fact from us. Next the idea of evolution was expressed in a poem by Erasmus Darwin. Then his grandson Charles marshaled the scientific evidence, and now today an army of pedants all over the world works on the bits and pieces of the idea. But when an idea has become so routinized with the pedants, there is a "*ricorso*" back to stage one and a new generation of crazies shocks us by talking of extraterrestrial intervention in human evolution. Thus we see a four-stage process: (1) Crazies; (2) Artists; (3) Savants; and (4) Pedants.

The work of von Däniken and the authors of *The Urantia Book* would be generally placed in the lunatic fringe of the world of ideas. But when we move from autodidactic von Däniken to autodidactic Doris Lessing, we have definitely crossed from stage one to stage two. It is not surprising that Doris Lessing could be a cell carrying new cosmic information, for she has always been something of a medium for the *Zeitgeist*. All the major themes of our time have found a place in her novels: war, communism, racism, feminism, mental illness, and now mysticism.

The novel *Briefing for a Descent into Hell* combines two major themes of Lessing's work, mental illness and apocalypse. The plot of the story is straightforward enough. A man is found wandering the streets of London; he is suffering from amnesia and is placed in a mental hospital. As two very different doctors (one good and one bad) try to minister to his needs, he is subjected to treatment by powerful drugs which only drive him deeper into sleep and dreams and madness. Even awake he remains in a trance, and with the lucidity of the mad, he answers the questions of his interrogators with a mind to the metaphysical puns contained in language seen in its denotative rather than its connotative function. The doctors, however, cannot step out of their ethnocentric limitations; as the thought police of the welfare state, they must take him into custody. Force is brought to bear with powerful drugs to bring him back into his proper culture. But the drugs only drive him deeper into his hallucination that he is a sailor on a raft. He had been on a yacht, but then a flying saucer, a "crystal," had come and taken his friends into heaven and left him behind. Singled out by the crystal, he singles himself out further by building a raft and abandoning the yacht. In this primitive vessel, he leaves society totally behind. He sails for countless time until finally he is beached on an island outside of time. If it was not clear whether the experience of the crystal was dream or experience, with the mysterious island it is now clear that we have left the simple metaphysics of objective world and subjective mind far behind. He has crossed over to that point where all dreams are experiences and all experience a dream.

On the island he is guided by two leopards (shades of the throne of the Great Mother of neolithic Anatolia!) to the top of a mountain plateau. Here he discovers the ruins of an ancient civilization, and in the square of the ceremonial center he discovers a circle which he intuitively recognizes as a landing place for the crystal. Scoured out by weeks of deprivation, he now hopes to be worthy of being carried into the sky. But when the crystal comes, he is again left behind; he cannot cross the barrier of the crystal's higher rate of vibration. So, abandoned by the gods, he takes up with savage hunters and wild beasts, to pass a cosmic season until once again, at the full of the moon, the crystal will descend. Like a god shipwrecked on the planet earth, he must join with its stream of evolution and wait out the Great Year until his fellow sons of God return.

He dwells as an alien among beasts and rat monkeys struggling to imitate men or gods by walking upright. It is clear from Lessing's quotations of Genesis 6:2–4 that she is implying that he is undergoing a repetition of the history of the earth. He watches beasts struggling to walk upright, and sees two going off by themselves, two whose auras give off a higher, finer light than the others. As we watch primates and savage hunters crisscrossing with visitors from another world, we see that the lines of evolution on this planet are not single or untouched by outside agitators. Here the novel reads like a variation on a theme from *The Urantia Book*, about which Lessing knows nothing, nor needs to, for she is nothing if not a medium for all the ideas flowing through the collective unconscious of our age.

The city was obviously built not by the savages but by the gods. Like Teotihuacán and ancient Uruk this is a city whose astronomical layout points toward the stars. Stranded in this ruin, he must wait out his cycle; he stays aloof from the wars of the beasts, but falls into one night of possession as he eats meat with the savages. And somehow this detour in the direction of the flesh prepares him for heaven, for when the crystal next returns, he is ready and is taken up like the apocryphal Enoch of old. As he looks out through the crystal, he "sees" the earth and knows it for the first time. Whatever failings the book has as a novel (and it is nowhere the novel that *The Golden Notebook* is), it is an incredible act of seership and clairvoyance. Lessing moves out of our conventional world view to see a different universe, a universe that is, in fact, the paradigm of the new science and the new world view of our emerging planetary culture. There is a tradition that the artist precedes the scientist in the examination of nature, and both Whitehead and Heisenberg maintain that it was the Renaissance artist whose close and detailed studies of nature laid the foundation for the empirical analyses of the scientific method.

As the hero ascends slowly in the crystal, he can see patternings of energy that were invisible before; those animals who are stronger and more highly evolved register on his sight; the others are invisible or foggy; the parts of the city which are strongest with this subtle energy show a glow in the stones. The very temples are built out of archetypal forms and formulas of universal structure, and, therefore, they resonate with the universe and redistribute subtle cosmic energies to the city.

I seemed to understand as I stood here in my new spritely shape that the areas of the city where the inner pattern was not strong enough to impose itself were where there was an extra heaviness and imperviousness in their substance. Whereas the parts of the city that were mirrored in the inner blueprint had as it were built into the stones a sample or portion of that fine inner light or substance.

This Atlantean city is the original, of which all others from Gizeh, to Stonehenge, to Teotihuacán are the copies. The stones are not mere rocks; they are crystals, and through their lattices flows a superconducting energy that holds information against the Second Law, and if someone stumbles upon them aeons later, someone who is karmically in affinity with their vibrations, then the information passes over to him and he hears voices or sees images or he is filled with a strongly intuitive, but imageless, sense of conviction. As he ascends higher, he sees that this etheric energy that flows through the stones forms a complete web of light circulating around the earth; it pours over the surface and seeks to find a way of moving from pure potential information to ideas realized in individual minds, but blocked by a culture of men who no longer understand the ancient cities, it can only find entrance in the remaining individuals who are attuned to it and can bring it down to earth.

The outer web of musical light created the inner earthly one and held it there in its dance of tension. And a scattering of people, a strand of them, a light webby tension of them everywhere over the globe, were the channels where the finer air went into the earth and fed it and kept it alive.

In the darkness that covered the earth these individuals and places were points of scattered light in a web which bound the dark. In an act of incredible mediumship, Lessing in her novelist's study was writing out in art what other people unknown to her were actually experiencing in different parts of the world.

But Lessing's clairvoyance does not stop at the discovery of lost civilizations and the web of etheric power points around the earth. The crystal goes higher to see the vibratory influence of the planets, called gods, on this wanderer, called earth. Intuiting the astronomical theories of Professor Hertha von Dechend, Lessing sees the wanderings of an Odysseus who is checked and frustrated by the gods to be an allegory of the earth wandering in its space checked by the forces of the planets. At its full height the crystal rests among the solar gods, and there the hero sees that the Fall was an historical event and that what is myth is truly the history of the earth. Unfortunately for the art of the book, Lessing loses her control of the novel at this point and *Briefing* becomes a tract re-visioning history and attacking the profession of archaeology.

The point of the re-visioning is to see the present crisis of earth in the light of the cataclysms that have destroyed the previous civilizations of lost time. The gods gather and decide to send yet another mission to the incorrigible planet, and, in illumination of the title of the book, a briefing is held to prepare them for their descent. The gods descend to become men, but to live among men they must lose all memory of their divinity. They will have to discover one another on earth, recover their memories through intuition, and piece together the members of the descent.

And so it becomes clear that Professor Charles Watkins, suffering from amnesia in a mental hospital in London, is really a god, or a part of a god. When his memory of being Charles Watkins is at its zenith, his memory of being a god is at its nadir. His lucid madness gives him a chance to recover his true memory. Before he was hospitalized other people began to recognize him and intuitively reassemble the members of the descent. But the good professor rejected them. And by the time the psychiatrists have done with him with their shock treatments, the "brain print" implanted by the gods during his briefing is erased. The classics professor is restored to his wife and family and his pedantic drudge of a department chairman. The mission to earth has failed. Now nothing stands between man and the end of his world. Like the novel before it, *Four-Gated City*, *Briefing* implies a bleak apocalyptic vision that the years remaining to this century are also the years remaining to our civilization.

Briefing for a Descent into Hell, like Carlyle's *Sartor Resartus*, is more of a personal vision than a novel; the voltage pours through the wires and burns up the thin insulation of the literary genre. Quite understandably, the literary critics have not made too much of the book, and were I a literary critic, I might not make much of the book either. But I for one could not afford the civilized luxury of literary criticism, for I was awestruck by the synchronicity of the book with my own life. Here Doris Lessing was writing a book about a professor of humanities who took a journey outside of time, discovered pieces of a lost civilization, and stumbled into the power points of the etheric web around earth. *Briefing* was published in the same month as *At the Edge of History*. We were writing out in different codes a message with the same structure. I could see why Doris Lessing would think that a professor would not stand a chance against the profession, and I could see why she would choose to veil her own thinking by putting it into the mouth of an imaginary character in a piece of fiction.

To turn away into a private space and then see your thoughts coming out in another's book, if only in *structure* and not in *texture* or content, is a strange experience. When I wrote to Doris Lessing and remarked on the synchronicity of her book and mine, she answered:

> It interests me, what you say about "synchronicity." It happens all the time. I have a private "funny" nightmare that one day I'll be inspired with a wonderful idea, sit down to write crying: "Eureka!," see the thing into print—and on the day it arrives in my hand will also arrive an absolutely identical book written by someone else. . . . But we don't really have to be like women afraid of being seen in public with dresses too alike. I just think ideas are "in the air" and get picked up by different people. . . .
>
> . . . I do find it particularly encouraging that you can write such books and yet be a professor at a university. That in itself is a sign of what you say: that we are on the edge of a move into a different way of looking at things.

When I first read *Briefing*, I had been mainly struck by the unorthodox theories of archaeology and their relation to my own work, but when I reread the novel some eighteen months and some twenty-eight thousand miles later, I saw that it was not only synchronistic with my life, but also prophetic. I had not fully appreciated the discussion of the etheric web of energy in the novel, but after coming back from Findhorn and discussions with David Spangler, I realized that her work was synchronistic with the work of others as well.

Something is carrying on an extended conversation,

through the opening and closing of our epochs, with the informational cells of our civilization. "Jesus People" would say it is Christ preparing for his Second Coming; pagans would say it is the return of the gods in their flying saucers; technologists would say, in the philosophy of Feuerbach, that it is not to the heavens we should look for an explanation, but to the earth: they themselves are the new gods who are ending the trivial culture of Homo Sapiens through genetic engineering. If we take all the variants of this planetary mythology, and try to sort out the information from the noise, we come up with four propositions of a new world view.

1. There is intelligent life in the universe beyond earth.
2. The meeting we are expecting in front of us in linear time has already occurred, is now occurring, and will continue to occur. The gods do not talk *to* us, they play *through* us *with* our history.
3. There is more to our history than the meager record of six thousand years. Our religious myths are the detritus of the lost history of earth.
4. Our subjective-objective distinctions about reality are incorrect. As in the world view of the Hopi Indians, Matter, Energy, and Consciousness form a continuum.

If one considers all the propositions of this planetary romanticism to be false, he can still take them seriously; at the very least, they can be seen as projections and caricatures of the large cultural shifts now occurring. Which of us has the power and mobility to go into all the laboratories, multinational corporation board rooms, and governmental cabinets to find out what is really going on on this planet? What the individual conscious ego does not know, however, does not limit the collective unconscious of mankind, and so one can make some intelligent guesses by paying attention to the seemingly unrelated works of art and mythologies at large.

As the old civilization of the industrial nation-states is

falling apart, it is also falling into new forms of a very old consciousness. Within this consciousness an ancient vision of reality is taking us into another dimension in which we can find our bearings once again to make the transition from civilization to planetization. Some god or *Weltgeist* has been making a movie out of us for the past six thousand years, and now we have turned a corner on the movie set of reality and have discovered the boards propping up the two-dimensional monuments of human history. The movement of humanism has reached its limit, and now at that limit it is breaking apart into the opposites of mechanism and mysticism and moving along the circumference of a vast new sphere of posthuman thought.

A new ideology is being created in advance of its social need; what particular institutional form this ideology will take no one can say. One cannot infer the Crystal Palace of the Great Exhibition of 1851 from the vision of the Scottish Primitivists of 1770. Perhaps it will take no institutional form at all, for it now seems that social institutions are no longer adequate vehicles of cultural evolution. We cannot go to church to find radiant Godhead, to the army to find glory in war, or to the universities to find aesthetic transfiguration or wisdom. Now only mysticism seems well suited to the post-institutional anarchism of technetronic culture, on the one hand, and the infinite posthuman universe on the other. The internal disciplines of the great mystical traditions seem to offer the only means by which man can feel at home in a universe so vast that, without the self-mastery and centering functions of meditation, he would go insane instantly.

Mystics think that they are solitary visionaries of God, but actually, in the transition from civilization to planetization, they have become the true political scientists. Mysticism seems impractical in technological culture because it is the dialectical negation of that culture and the affirmation of the next culture. Gardening was impractical in hunting culture when busy men of affairs had to be on the move in search of game, and that is why it remained for women to transform food-gathering into agriculture. Stone Age men were too busy with their elaborate tools to create the dazzlingly more simple and advanced civilization based upon agriculture. Now, once again, man is too busy with his elaborate tools to create the even more dazzlingly simple and advanced planet-ization. But at least one practical-minded economist, Kenneth Boulding, recognizes the new human possibilities.

Now if we look around us today to see what in man's experience looks like the foreshadowing of things to come, we may well find it in the experience of the mystics and the gropings of man in religion. It will be surprising indeed if man as we know him today represented the total exhaustion of all evolutionary potential.[11]

These remarks by a Western economist should be compared with the thoughts of the two Indian yogis, Sri Aurobindo and Gopi Krishna:

Life evolves out of Matter, Mind out of Life, because they are already involved there: Matter is a form of veiled Life, Life a form of veiled Mind. May not Mind be a form and veil of a higher power, the Spirit, which would be supramental in its nature? Man's highest aspiration would then only indicate the gradual unveiling of the Spirit within, the preparation of a higher life upon earth.[12]

On the basis of my own experience, extending to more than thirty years, I have come to the conclusion that mankind is slowly evolving towards a sublime state of consciousness of which fleeting glimpses have been afforded to us by all great seers and mystics of the past and present.[13]

It is certainly paradoxical to see an economist looking to the mystic for the cultural evolution of man, but there are many paradoxes in the dialectical process of history. As one looks at the mirror-images bouncing off one another, it would seem that for every thought there is an equal and opposite action. Religions that are created to liberate us end up controlling us; technologies that are created to rationalize us end up by mystically stimulating us. The railroads stimulated the appearance of the hobo; television stimulated the appearance of the Yippie. In each case it was the man who rejected the society of technology who, again paradoxically, became the artistic master of that technology. To work "within the system" of a technology is to be turned into a functionary of the tool; to wield a tool one must grasp it from the outside. This is why Buckminster Fuller has said that "The big thinking in general—of a spherical earth and celestial navigation, in contradistinction to a four-cornered flat world with only localized preoccupations—was retained exclusively by the great pirates." And so it was in 1968: in an electronic-media society the Yippies were pirates of the news. With a consummate display of political ability, they stood outside the political parties and stole the Democratic Convention away from the functionaries dominated by the system. And so it was in the nineteenth century: while a Casey Jones or a Huntington Hartford could make a great noise and seem to be a hero of the new technology of the railroads, he was really a victim. The only one who humanistically mastered the whole cultural system of the rails was the hobo riding a few inches above them. While most Americans were still locked into the ethos of the small town, the hobo had moved out to a continental frame of reference.

But the knave is not the only one to stand outside the society of technology. Since the time of Moses desert places have been filled with both outlaws and saints, and Moses himself was both. Today there are many who stand outside the society of technology, but once again those who make the loudest noise are not always its masters. The hippies claimed to be the masters of chemistry and electronics—and fast became their victims. Now the technocrats and university professors are claiming to be the masters of the new technology. But once again the paradox is holding true: the technology intended to rationalize us is actually mystically stimulating us—witness Apollo 17. The professors produce over one million scientific papers a year, so many that no one can process information *rationally* any more. Like Casey Jones, who must drive harder and harder, the professors have become the victims of their own technology. Now the only one who has mastered educational technology through supra-rational modes of consciousness is the man on the outside, the mystic. While the scientist may look on his meters and oscilloscope—recording body temperature and brain waves— it is the yogi at the other end of the line who is experiencing joy at the speed of illumination.

All through evolution man has survived because he remained generalized and adaptable. He did not grow a claw on his arm; he held a tool and put it aside when he was finished with it. Now our tools are not single objects, but an entire culture of technology and management. We are not free to drop the culture of technology and move on to something else, because now the culture is trying to grow on its own terms by adapting *us* to *it*. The mechanists wish to alter human nature to make the vestigial ape in man fit for life in a technological society; the mystics wish to change man through consciousness and "kundalini, the evolutionary energy." For both Faust and Buddha there is no such thing as normalcy; the green earth at its best is still a cosmic playpen.

The mechanist and the mystic may be opposites in content, but they are not opposites in structure, because cultures progress dialectically: they break into the opposing forces that are in collusion with one another to end the old and bring in the new. The romantic artist like Shelley and the industrial engineer like Brunel were the opposites of the nineteenth century, but in their striving to build bridges to the sky they were much closer to one another than to the squire and peasant of an eighteenth-century village. So it is now with the mechanist and the mystic. Humanists and ecologists want to make the earth comfortable to their bodies, but the mechanists are destroying the earth as fast as an insect destroys its cocoon. And though mystics may not build factories, they seem just as intent on regarding the death of earth as the birth of the new cosmic man. In this respect, Teilhard de Chardin's vision is remarkably close to the ending of Arthur C. Clarke's *Childhood's End*.

Let us suppose from this universal centre, this Omega Point, there constantly emanate radiations hitherto only perceptible to those persons we call "mystics." Let us further imagine that, as the sensibility or response to mysticism of the human race increases with planetisation, the awareness of Omega becomes so widespread as to warm the earth psychically while physically it is growing cold. Is it not conceivable that Mankind, at the end of its totalisation, its folding-in upon itself, may reach a critical level of maturity where, leaving the earth and stars to lapse slowly back into the dwindling mass of primordial energy, it will detach itself from this planet and join the one true, irreversible essence of things, the Omega Point? A phenomenon perhaps outwardly akin to death; but in reality a simple metamorphosis and arrival at the supreme synthesis.[14]

Père Teilhard envisioned this convergence toward the Omega Point as far off in the future, but if we look at the population graph of mankind from 2,000,000 B.C. to A.D. 2000, we see an asymptotic curve that comes to a point twenty-six years from now when the earth's population is to reach seven billion. And as one looks back over the curve, he sees that space-time has begun to contract around us.[15] Before, cultural transformations occurred over hundreds of thousands of years; then, over thousands of years in the Neolithic Revolution; then, over centuries in the Industrial Revolution; and now, in the Technetronic Revolution, the transformation is occurring over mere decades. No individual ever witnessed the Neolithic Revolution, and only a few sensitive individuals in the eighteenth century witnessed the Industrial Revolution, but now the individual life span is long enough, and the cultural transformation short enough, that solitary man can become conscious of mankind in a way only the mystics knew before. We are the climactic generation of human cultural evolution, and in the microcosm of our lives the macrocosm of the evolution of the human race is playing itself out: which is exactly what our new mythologies (like 2001) are trying to tell us.

Now as human culture seems to be accelerating to the speed of light, it does seem, in proper Einsteinian fashion, as if our mass were expanding to infinity. Cultures move through the medium of time as airplanes move through the medium of air, so it is no wonder that both the mechanists and the mystics are trying to streamline the design of human culture. But our culture is so wholly novel that it seems to be affecting the very nature of time itself. Clearly, some death or rebirth of man is not as far off as Teilhard imagined. Because human culture is coming to a point, the distance between the edges of good and evil seems to be narrowing. The multinational corporations are devoted to profits and the exploitation of resources; nevertheless, they are creating structures for planetization. They are also accelerating the ecological death of the planet, and this in turn is accelerating the mystical transformation of mankind by stimulating the appearance of a new religious sensibility.

Under the threat of species annihilation, Homo Sapiens is trying to accomplish its transformation into a new species. Since aeons ago man made his own culture into the vehicle of his evolution, the appearance of this new species is to be found not in individual babies with three eyes in their heads but in the cultural vehicle itself. The mechanist works in great contempt for human nature and hopes to improve the race through genetic engineering and electronic manipulation of the brain; the mystic avoids the Faustian pathology of the mechanist and regards machines as crude metaphors for the real powers of the spirit. As Sri Aurobindo has said: "Much that can now only be known, worked out, or created by the use of invented tools and machinery might be achieved by the new body in its own power or by the inhabitant spirit through its own direct spiritual force."[16] But in walking away from the culture of technology, the mystic spirals back in the direction of the past and up to the posttechnological culture of the future. In a phenomenology of opposites there is an exchange of characteristics in which the mystic becomes the new political scientist and the mechanist becomes the solitary laboratory man cut off from his fellow men in pursuit of some alien vision.

As the technologist becomes increasingly alienated from the realities of contemporary culture, he will refuse to accept the disconfirmation of his vision of man's control of nature and will hysterically try to reassert his power. Social scientists (like Professor Leon Festinger) who have studied occultists have shown that "when prophecy fails," the prophets refuse to accept the evidence, but instead try even harder to prove the validity of their views by seeking the affirmation of converts. But this knowledge can cut both ways, esoteric and exoteric. Now that the technocratic prophets of progress are suffering from "cognitive dissonance," they are rejecting the disconfirmation of their position and calling for more power. In 1967 Herman Kahn wrote his book about *The Year 2000*; but it wasn't even as far ahead as 1968, since it had absolutely nothing to say about pollution. Predictably, Kahn has not learned his lesson; now he is calling for futurologists to deal with the future of pollution. While technologists can't be expected to turn themselves into Hopi Indians, they can adopt a view of reality appropriate to the situation instead of calling for more infections to cure the disease. Having destroyed the environment, the technologists of the multinational corporations will want to move us into domed cities, the company towns of the planetary era, where the ape's attachment to nature can be eliminated from man by scientific means. Since technological man cannot live in the universe, the retreat from nature need not stop with the dome; he can go on to the electronic drawer. With electronic probes implanted directly in the brain, man will not have to endure the pain, anxiety, and accidents of the sensorimotor life; by bypassing the senses, man can have a completely programmed life of intense physical pleasure and yet never have to leave his drawer. Like the loved ones of Forest Lawn, technological man in his psychedelic sarcophagus will have the best that his culture can give him.

But the most immediate danger of our technological system of management is that it is interfering with the movements of cultural evolution that are making man ready for planetization. As long as mechanism is checked by mysticism, and as long as planetary technology is checked by planetary mythology, as it was in Apollo 17, the dialectic works out and the Pythagorean synthesis of mysticism and science is possible; but if one wins out over the other, we will have a linear reduction of the wave. The future is in neither the world-denying asceticism of India nor the world-destroying industrialism of America. Just as once Pythagoras took the East into Greece to create the foundation of Western civilization, so has his spirit returned to take India into America to create the foundation of our earthly planetization.

The Pythagoreans are few and the Archimedeans are many, but perhaps Apocalypse will take care of mechanistic positivism. As long as things are going fine, the positivist praises progress and seems well adjusted to reality; but in times of suffering and catastrophe his optimism flips into its linked opposite in pessimism and misanthropic bitterness. Only the tragic sense of life is capable of sustaining an enduring strength and joy. It was this religious sense of tragedy that saw the blacks through three hundred years of slavery, the Irish through seven hundred years of captivity, and the Jews through millennia of persecution. Now that the confident positivism of the technologist has brought us to the edge, it will take the vision of the mystics to see us through.

And we will have much to go through. If we are experiencing a change in the cultural vehicle of human evolution, and a new kind of man is emerging, then it is not likely that the old man will willingly disinherit himself. When a culture is at the edge of extinction, it explodes, like the seed from a hanged man, into primitive seminal movements that try to make a new life for the dying culture through a desperate "simplification through intensity." If Middle America attacked the young for rejecting its middle-class life style, one can imagine the scope of persecution leveled against men who reject their species' life. Perhaps that is why the Hopi Indians and artists like Doris Lessing and Arthur C. Clarke see the evolutionary mutants being taken away by the gods. According to some Hopi prophecies, the earth's magnetic field will reverse and the sun's radiation will burn out the dense undergrowth in preparation for a new planting of the racially hybrid, planetized man.

But if mankind is a single de Broglie wave, then not one individual should fall without the entirety rushing to pick him up and carry him on. The remorseless vision of conflict and destruction is more Homeric than Christian, so perhaps now that we have reached the limit of Western Christian civilization, we need to understand the civilization that we are about to leave behind. If the ego with its passionate hatreds is a form of blindness, and mankind is a single interpenetrating field, then Dante's *"l'amor che muove il sole e l'altre stelle"* is more than metaphor. Perhaps in the spiral of time there is an occult closeness between primitive Christianity and contemporary anarchist Christianity, and at the intersection of myth and history only a union of contradictory opposites can express the truth beyond institutionalization. In the union of the California hip movement with the fundamentalist traditions of rural America, there is the hopeful sign that the new decentralizing informational technology has helped to overcome the dreary split between avant-garde and hick backlash that has characterized the thinking of an America dominated by an urban and sophisticated elite. Since it was the urban revolution of six thousand years ago that first split human culture into urban and rural values,[17] perhaps now that we are beginning to live in global villages, we are beginning to overcome the habits of mind of the millennia of civilized man.

Since religion has always been about what lies beyond the container of urban civilization, I doubt if we have come to the end of man's religious experience. In fact, only man's religious myths have been thinking on a scale large enough to deal with what is happening. If man is coming to the end of hominization, the next step in human evolution cannot be simply another tool added to a list that stretches from fist-hatchets to computers. The next step will be like the transformation that altered an ape into a man, and looking at our planetary mythologies, we can see that this is what we have been waiting for.

SEVEN

To Findhorn and Lindisfarne

I did not know why I had picked Lindisfarne out of all the monastery schools of the Dark Ages, and I did not know what I would do when I got there; but I went on all the same. When after nearly three months of traveling I finally came to Holy Island off the coast of Northumbria, I had only a few minutes to cross before the tide flooded the channel. I was glad that I had followed my hunch not to stop on the way down from Edinburgh, for now I would have the whole afternoon on the island until the channel again opened at dusk. I crossed over quickly, parked the car, and began a slow psychic ambulation in search of whatever was left. I circled around the castle on the high rock, went down to the shore, paced in the enclosed garden, and came back to the ruin of the twelfth-century priory and the modern chapel. Nothing of the original seventh-century monastery remained; after the sacred power of the founding saints had gone, the profane power of the Danes had come in like the tides. Since there was no other place in which to meditate, I went into the modern chapel. In all the sacred places that I had visited, from Ryoanji to Eleusis, I made an attempt to gather them up in consciousness, as if in the spiral of planetary culture we had to look back to all the religions of the past and then move beyond them to the next level of our religious evolution. I decided that if I did my kriya in the chapel I would be visualizing a circle, a mandala around the earth. Yogananda had brought Kriya Yoga from India to Los Angeles half a century ago; I had grown up in Los Angeles, but had taken the four-year course in Kriya Yoga during my retreat in Canada, and now I was preparing to return to America. By visualizing the circle going around India, California, and Holy Island, and by doing my kriya in the chapel, I could bring an internal contemplative technique back to a place steeped in the anarchist Christianity that had come to the Celts from out of the monastery traditions of Egypt.

Once I had concluded my meditation, I had only to wait until the tide went out to return to Edinburgh. In the chapel I bought a little pamphlet that told of the life of St. Aidan, the founder of Lindisfarne, and of St. Cuthbert, his greatest successor. One of the stories seemed to connect the spirit of Lindisfarne with the esoteric traditions of ancient desert Judaism. According to the point of view of Yogananda, John the Baptist was the reincarnation of Elijah, and Jesus was the reincarnation of Elijah's disciple, Elisha. When Elisha asks his departing guru that a double part of his spirit may descend upon him, he is asking for an acceleration of his spiritual evolution. Elijah cannot grant this to him, for it can only take place if Elisha himself can stand to take it all at once. And so Elijah tells him that if he can control his consciousness perfectly so as to be able to see him ascend through all the planes of consciousness (*lokas*), then Elisha's own mastery will be achieved. Elisha does see Elijah ascend to heaven in a fiery chariot; he picks up the mantle of Elijah and returns to the Mt. Carmel ashram and all the followers recognize that Elisha now wears the power and mantle of Elijah. A similar kind of prophetic succession is expressed in the hagiography of Aidan and Cuthbert.

On the night of St. Aidan's death an athletic lad of 17, whose dust is now the prized possession of Durham Cathedral, where his name—CUTHBERTUS—is engraved on a great stone slab behind the high altar, was watching sheep in the Leader valley on the lower slopes of the Lammermoor hills. Awake while other shepherds were sleeping, he had a vision of angels bearing a great soul to paradise; and when a few days later news came of the death of the beloved Aidan, he took the vision as a call to the services of God.[1]

It would seem that much of the esoteric was transmitted to archaic Celtic Christianity; or, perhaps, it would be closer to the truth to say that in Ireland two streams met to create the river that sustained life in Western Europe in the Dark Ages. One was the ancient stream of esoteric thought that had been centered in primeval Ireland since time out of mind; the other was the modern Christian stream which had its source in that other fountainhead of esoteric traditions, Egypt.[2] With Druid Ireland on one side and syncretistic Egypt on the other, we can see that there is really only one universal esoteric knowledge for the transformation of consciousness. Whether it is the Indian snake of kundalini, or the Egyptian serpent rising out of the forehead, or the Mexican plumed serpent, or the winged snakes of the caduceus of Mercury, or the serpent worship of the Druid priesthood that St. Patrick drove out of Ireland, it is all part of the same mystery. Of course, most scholars won't accept such Pynchonesque scholarship, but you can imagine that if our civilization were to be wiped out, no scholar a thousand years from now would be willing to accept the fact that pieces of things as different as Volkswagens, Cadillacs, and buses all represented, not isolated cultures, but parts of one industrial civilization that covered the face of the earth. They would split it all up in tiny pieces and talk about how the Volkswagen I people conquered the Ford II people until both were replaced by an empire which moved people in large vehicles. Other scholars would argue that no one could possibly have crossed the great ocean, and that the Ford and Volkswagen cultures had nothing to do with one another but were separate and independent inventions.

Men traveled in ancient times as they travel now, carrying their culture with them in their heads. Pythagoras was not the first or the last man to travel and bring the mysteries of the East to the West. Strange as it may seem, St. Cuthbert seemed to know the yoga of body heat and how to match the waves of inhalation and exhalation with mantras and waves of the sea.

A spying monk recorded how he watched him descend the cliff while others were sleeping, cross the slippery rocks, enter the sea, and chant psalms while the waves lapped around him; and how on his return to shore two small creatures, otters or young seals, came and rubbed themselves upon his chilled feet.[3]

It is sad to think how little of the esoteric has survived in Christianity, and how we must go the whole length of the world to find something as simple as a breathing technique for quieting the mind so that we may enter states of consciousness deeper than the exoteric prayers of give-me-this and give-me-that. Americans have to go to the "New Religions" because our old religions of Catholic, Protestant, and Jew can give us only the institutional culture of religion and not the experience of God. Professor Jacob Needleman has been eloquent in his diagnosis:

This general forgetting of the instrumental nature of religious forms is in a way really quite bizarre. It is as though millions of people suffering from a painful disease were to gather together to hear someone read a textbook of medical treatment in which the means necessary to cure their disease were carefully spelled out. It is as though they were all to take great comfort in that book and in what they heard, going through their lives knowing that their disease could be cured, quoting passages to their friends, preaching the wonders of this great book, and returning to the congregation from time to time to hear more of the inspiring diagnosis and treatment read to them. Meanwhile, of course, the disease worsens and they eventually die of it, smiling in grateful hope as on their deathbed someone reads to them yet another passage from the text. Perhaps for some a troubling thought possesses their minds as their eyes close for the last time: "Haven't I forgotten something? Something important? Haven't I forgotten actually to undergo treatment?"[4]

Christianity once contained specific instructions on the cure of the disease, but these instructions about techniques of inner consciousness opened doors that were not the doors of the Church with its clergy and sacraments, so the doors were slammed shut in a campaign carried on over centuries to wipe out "heretics." No doubt the Princes of the Church were able to terrorize a few monks and nuns with the examples of a few psychotics, and, perhaps, a few of these psychotic heretics were really evil; but if Christianity had kept the esoteric tradition alive, there would have been, as well as Popes and Cardinals, a few adepts who knew the inner geography of the soul sufficiently well to tell the spirit of the Lord from possession by the devil.

But it is pointless now to argue over whose fault it was. We have to accept the fact that we now live in a time when the esoteric traditions of Christianity are dead, and the esoteric traditions of Western science are fast dying, so that the whole light of the civilization that came out of Christian Europe is flickering toward a new age of darkness. Now we live in a culture in which the mystical science of Kepler, Descartes, Pascal, and Newton has been reduced to the university departments of social science, in a culture in which the Christianity of Columba, Aidan, and Cuthbert has been reduced to the soporific pieties of a bureaucracy of sanctimonious clerks. The esoteric is not living in Christianity, and, as Professor Needleman has pointed out:

> The esoteric is the heart of human civilization. And should the outward forms of a human civilization become totally unable to contain and adapt the energies of great spiritual teachings, then that civilization has ceased to serve its function in the universe.[5]

Not only has it ceased to serve its function, but it has cut itself off from the very universal energies with which it could maintain its life.

If you wish to go back to the point at which Christianity took the wrong turn, so that you can find the other road at the fork, you must go back to Lindisfarne to see the clash between the esoteric Christianity of Jesus and John and the ecclesiastical Christianity *about* Jesus but *of* Peter and Paul.

The clash had been developing during the episcopate of Finan, who succeeded Aidan at Lindisfarne; and it became unavoidable when Oswy in 655 slew Penda of Mercia, the last defender of heathenism, who had stood between the stream of Christianity coming down from Iona and the stream pressing northwards from Canterbury. Colman, the third bishop, inherited the dispute when Finan died in 661. King Oswy's sympathies were with the Celtic Church in which he had been brought up at Iona, but his queen and her chaplain followed the usages they had been familiar with in Kent. The confusion in the royal household was such that Easter was kept twice. . . . The king's long reign (642–670) and religious zeal gave the Church the opportunity to become deeply rooted in his extensive kingdom; but which Church and which customs was he to support? Aware that the Easter divergence in 665 would be even greater than usual, Oswy summoned the Synod of Whitby in 663 or 664 at the monastery ruled by Hilda, pleading that all who served the one God should agree to observe one rule of life. Colman claimed that the Celtic traditions went back to St. John; but Wilfrid, a former disciple of Aidan, who had visited Rome and adopted Roman usages, laid emphasis on the folly of resisting the unique authority of St. Peter: "The only people who are stupid enough to disagree with the whole world are these Scots and their obstinate adherents the Picts and the Britons, who inhabit only a portion of these two islands in the remote ocean." The king had evidently already made up his mind, with a view to unity and peace in his own house, and with a smile he announced his decision in these words: "If Peter is the guardian of the gates of heaven, I shall not contradict him. I shall obey his commands in everything to the best of my ability: otherwise, when I come to the gates of heaven, he who holds the key may not be willing to open them."[6]

Two roads crossed at Lindisfarne; one went to Rome through Wilfrid, the other went to Iona through Colman. Aidan had come to Lindisfarne from Iona, and it was at Iona that Aidan's teacher, St. Columba, had created a center of esoteric Christianity. It is small wonder that after the failures of the Synod of Whitby Colman and his monks left Lindisfarne and went back to remote Iona. It would be nice if we, too, could go back to Iona to find some old document like the Book of Kells that would give us instruction in Christian forms of meditation, but the inner techniques are rarely committed to writing. They pass from realized man to realized man, and if we are to rediscover them in the present, it is not to some exercise in archaeology that we must commit ourselves but to those living places where the culture of man is not cutting violently against the grain of the universe.

We have been so turned around by our society that we no longer feel the stars turn. We have become so used to feeling religious only when we are uncomfortable and full of pride for having bothered to go to church at all that we no longer remember that religion was once a force that created civilization out of barbarism and inspired almost all the great works of art in history. The power of cosmic myth is still with us, but it is not to be found in churches or elegant drawing rooms where clerics and academics sip sherry and discuss a fine point in the latest fashions of theology. When the unconscious and the conscious come together in a culture, the energies are not polite, civilized, or comforting. It is one thing to toast the Queen at high table, and quite another to dance with a live rattlesnake in your mouth at Oraibi, or walk on fire in New Guinea, or commune with devas in Findhorn.

These places are most foreign to us, and to walk into them is to walk into another culture in another age. One of the most foreign of them all is not hidden away in the Himalayan fastness of Tibet or the upper reaches of the Amazon, but in the middle of a trailer park an hour's drive outside of Inverness in Scotland.

I had first heard of Findhorn just a day before beginning the trip around the world. I was visiting Professor Alistair Taylor of Queen's University in Ontario for the first time, and as we began to become acquainted with one another, he kept testing me to see how far out I would go in various matters of the occult. Having satisfied himself and his wife Mary that I was reasonably far-out, he decided upon the ultimate test. Mary Taylor arose and went into the other room and came out with my final examination papers, some literature on Findhorn. She explained that in the previous year they had visited this community in Findhorn Bay where the people communicated with devas, elves, sprites, elementals, extraterrestrial minds, and God Almighty Himself; but most specifically their ruling *genius loci* seemed to enable them to grow vegetables practically out of sand. I had heard about Cleve Backster's research in New York concerning the stimulation of plant growth through love and conversation, but this was a good deal farther out than talking to your geraniums to make them grow big and strong. For all my Irish ancestry and my mother's talk of banshees, I began to have a suspicion that Professor and Mrs. Taylor had indeed outdone me. But as I picked up the literature and began to browse through it, my feelings began to change. Asking to borrow the pamphlets, I decided to take them home and read them through.

And what I read that night stopped me cold. The community emphasized that we were now living in a New Age and that this New Age had begun on midnight of December 31, 1967. Now that date and that precise hour had marked a very important turning point in my life. A few days before New Year's Eve I felt a very strong intuitive prompting, a voice if you will, that told me that on New Year's Eve I was not to go out celebrating, I was to stay home and be in the meditative state as midnight came and one year passed into another. That was all very well, except for the fact that I did not really know how to meditate. I had tried when I was sixteen to meditate without formal instruction and failed; I did not make another attempt until the summer of 1967. I had tried to meditate using Edward Maupin's Esalen pamphlet, but got nowhere; then I tried some Zen breathing techniques and made a little progress toward being able to sit still for fifteen minutes or so. But that progress was not sufficient to follow the instructions of the intuitive prompting; still, I knew better than to ignore my intuition. And so on New Year's Eve I stayed home and went into my study to meditate before midnight. That night my meditation was quieter and deeper than it had ever been before. I had no words, voices, or concepts to deal with what was going on in me, or where or how, but I could feel my life turning. A few days later I began to prepare to leave MIT. My Canadian retreat was about to begin.

When I was living in Toronto in 1968, a friend said that the lessons put out by the Yogananda Ashram were not half bad. Since we both had grown up in Los Angeles, there was a bemused tone in the grudging recognition. I had driven by the golden lotus shrines of the Self-Realization Fellowship on Sunset Boulevard countless times, but to me they were just part of the general Hollywood movie-set approach to the "wisdom of the East." I was repelled by the architecture, the Westerners with Sanskrit names, and SRF's middle-aged churchy approach to yoga. As an apostate Catholic, I wanted no more of churches. I had been interested in yoga in high school, and when I dropped out of L.A. High, I spent much of my time reading the classical texts of Eastern mysticism and going to lectures at one occult society after another; and out of all those lectures the most impressive one was a talk on meditation given by a follower of Yogananda. The man clearly embodied everything he was talking about, so I should have enrolled then and not waited another fourteen years. But I was sixteen, and the Modigliani vision of "une vie brève mais intense" had a hold on me. So I read *A Portrait of the Artist* and skipped *The Autobiography of a Yogi*.

But by the time I was thirty I had seen enough of the "sickies" who were poets and novelists. With some personal experience in the stupidity of turning the body into a funeral pyre to find some illumination, I was more ready to accept the architecture of SRF and the awful poems by Yogananda at the head of each weekly lesson. There were still times when the intellectual in me objected and thought how much better it would be to start each lesson with a poem by Traherne, Vaughan, St. John of the Cross, or Rumi, but I winced at Yogananda's mixed metaphors and kept on with the four-year course. Sylvia Plath could write better poetry than Yogananda, but I was not interested in following her. After a year of following Yogananda's path, the experiences in meditation overwhelmed and silenced the silly fussings of my snobbish tastes.

And so as I read over the literature from Findhorn I began

to see that all the experiences of my years in Canada had come out of that midnight of December 31, 1967. If that night had transformed both Findhorn and myself, then I would have to follow the connections to their source.

On my way to Inverness on the train up from Edinburgh I shared a table at lunch with a young Scottish university student. We talked of universities and travel, and as we compared our summers, he was amazed that anyone who had seen some of the wonders of the world would bother to go to the little village of Findhorn. He couldn't believe that anything interesting could be going on in his own backyard. And that attitude seemed typical: Findhorn was becoming famous in the international counterculture, but the villagers of Findhorn hardly knew of its existence.

You could see why, for you could drive right by it without ever noticing it; and even if you did see the sign for "THE FINDHORN BAY CARAVAN PARK," it would be hard to imagine a more unpoetic setting for a "New Age" planetary community. The only place that could be less poetic than a caravan park in Findhorn was a trailer park in El Monte, California. Swept by gale winds in the winter, and surrounded by sand dunes and scrub grass in the summer, the place was no rival for Esalen or Tassajara in Big Sur. Peter Caddy, the founder of Findhorn, had often passed the caravan park and remarked to his wife what an awful place it would be to live.

Peter could afford the luxury of feeling superior to the place when he had a good job running an attractive hotel nestled in a valley by the side of Cluny Hill. But when those days were gone and he was a middle-aged man out of a job and having a rather mysteriously frustrating time in finding work, he could no longer afford to be superior, only surprised when he and his wife Eileen and their friend Dorothy found themselves living in a caravan plunked down in just that park. And, as if that wasn't bad enough, for good measure they were given the plot next to the garbage dump. By the side of a garbage dump in a trailer park on a bleak dune in the northern reaches of Scotland, a planetary town of the Age of Aquarius was to be born: no Oraibi on an Arizona mesa overlooking miles of mountain and desert; no Big Sur with redwood forests, mountain cliffs, and Pacific Ocean; no Mount Shasta hollowed out by extraterrestrials to hide their flying saucers, and forget about Tibet or the cities hidden in the other dimensions of the Bermuda Triangle.

I parked my VW and began to wander among the trailers and prefabricated bungalows in search of the office. The vibrations of the place were good, but there was nothing mysterious and overwhelming. When you walked into the "Good Guest House" of the Sri Aurobindo Ashram, a wave of peace swept over you that was as palpable as the humidity coming in from the Bay of Bengal. But here the tone was light, very relaxed and informal. The people walking about seemed to be working quite normally, and not one of them was talking to a plant. I asked directions to the office, introduced myself to Peter Caddy, and referred him to the letter I had written from Canada. Peter found the letter, reread it, and then gave me a long, hard, scrutinizing stare with those steel-blue ice eyes of his. After the visual examination was over, the oral examination began, and Peter said in a most headmasterly fashion: "You must tell me exactly what it is you are here for. If we are to help, we must know precisely what you are interested in." I explained something of my December 31, 1967, and the purpose of my trip here to Lindisfarne and Findhorn, and then I said that I would give him some materials on the Lindisfarne Association, which I was starting up in New York.

Peter seemed satisfied, invited me to tea at five, and gave me my visitor's form to fill out. It asked for a description of whatever skills you had. I put down cooking, but I was told later with a chuckle that the people who came to Findhorn more often put down things like: aura scanning, psychic healing, psychometrizing, deva communication, astral projection, water-witching, and eckankar.

I was assigned a room slightly larger than a coffin in a trailer, and a very friendly woman set me up with towels, tea, and sugar. She was not your common spaced-out head, but a more classic Briton whom you could imagine asking you in to have a nice cup of tea; but if I thought I was going to lock onto an identity for the place that quickly, I was soon proven wrong by a couple of long-haired American kids who were working around the trailer. With her on one side and the kids on the other, Findhorn was unlike any commune I could think of in the States.

When I went into the dining room for dinner that evening, this quality of opposites became even more apparent. The dining room was filled with handmade plank tables and benches and reminded me of Esalen; but the people, unlike those at Esalen, were of all types and classes, hair lengths and accents: crew-cut, medium, and shoulder length; Blackpool, Scots, U and non-U, and American. The food was organic and vegetarian and good; and if the style was hip Californian, the atmosphere was not: no trash, no dirty kids running around screaming, and no dope. There seemed to be no obvious rules, no compulsory silence at meals, no cosmic seriousness, just laughter and relaxation.

After dinner and the cleaning up, the community retired into a room they called the "Sanctuary" for fifteen minutes of silent meditation and a talk by a young American named David Spangler. The room was small and held only about forty or fifty armless but upholstered chairs arranged in semicircles facing the single decoration in the room, a simple hand-woven tapestry of a radiant cross. There was no particular seating arrangement; people came to Sanctuary, left their shoes in the outer room, and then went in to sit in silence. Some of the young Americans preferred to sit in the lotus position to meditate in full yogic fashion, but others preferred to pray or sit simply in the silence. Peter told me later that Findhorn was not a meditation center, that those who wished to spend long hours in meditation were encouraged to go to the nearby Tibetan center; Findhorn was a place for living and working together. The subtle blending of energies, auras, and thoughts in Sanctuary morning and night was all that was asked by way of a formal contemplative discipline. In the philosophy of Findhorn: "The day of study and retreat is past. We must balance our cerebrations and meditations with down-to-earth externalization and anchoring of the New Age visions."

After the period of silence, David Spangler began to speak. If Peter Caddy was the forceful man of action and organization, a combination of the tweedy headmaster and the retired RAF officer, David Spangler was his opposite. Peter was the Headman and David was the Shaman. Dressed casually in his blue turtleneck, David with his sandy hair and boyish face looked too young to be giving sermons; but it seems that at twenty-seven he had already put in ten years of public speaking. David had dropped out of a science major at the University of Arizona to follow an intuitive calling to study the esoteric, and now in his twenties he was a philosopher in the tradition of a Rudolf Steiner. David's style was not flashy or charismatic, but slow and thoughtful, and filled with many pauses that seemed to be part of a rhythm that went with the flow of his words; but as he spoke, something would happen to him, and some of his sentences would come out with a totally different quality. You could almost hear the "clunk" of a gear falling into place as his mind went into spiritual overdrive, and a new power began flowing out of him. He spoke without notes and the general direction of his thought was straightforward enough, but in momentary digressions he would toss off outrageously fascinating points that you would want him to spend the whole hour on. And he could joke in a very light and whimsical way as he went along. People actually laughed in Sanctuary! By comparison with other satsangs in many spiritual groups around the world, the Findhorn Sanctuary was very unpretentious. They could move from absolute seriousness on an apocalyptic level to lighthearted whimsey. Here was none of your white-eyeballed six-chakra neon, saffron robes and incense, flat-out pranams, or red carpets for the lotus feet of his exalted cosmic satguruship. The people relaxed, laughed, and let visitors find their own way; there were no heavy indoctrinations or recitations from the catechism or the party line.

After David's talk a group of visitors was taken back to the community center to see a slide presentation called "This Is Findhorn." The quality of the photography and the audio editing was exceptional; with its dissolve techniques and its sound-on-sound, the presentation was light-years away from the smudgy inked mimeographed communications of many occult societies. And the musical background for the tape recording was also hard to believe. When I was told that Findhorn had a folk singing group which wrote its own songs, I prepared myself for moral rearmament hymns and "up-lifting" numbers. But what I heard was really fine; the girls' voices blended exceptionally well, the songs were good, and a few of them were very good—on a par with Joni Mitchell or Simon and Garfunkel. The place, it seemed, was loaded with talent. They had sound engineers, photographers, musicians, song writers, actors, singers, a string quartet, candlemakers, potters, weavers, and cooks. When I had first read about Findhorn at the Taylors' house, I had had visions of plump middle-aged women in flowered dresses calling on the spirits of the dear-departed and with rhinestones on squat fingers levitating one leg of a piece of Chippendale. But listening to the songs and the guitars, it was hard to believe that I wasn't back home in California.

The next morning I was given a tour of Findhorn by John

Hilton, an ex-banker from London who had been a student of the teachings of Gurdjieff. John had a very clear and bright tone; he stood very straight and his face wore an alert smile as if he was doing something he keenly enjoyed. With his years of banking experience, there was a no-nonsense air to him, so you couldn't ask for a more rational guide to the mysteries of Findhorn. I was shown the craft centers: the studios for candlemaking, pottery, weaving, and painting; and the print shop where David's book, *Revelation for a New Age,* had just been published. After the tour we went back to John's bungalow to have coffee (yes, I said coffee and not mint tea) with his wife, Mary. Mary Hilton was a musician and the conductor of Findhorn's choral society and madrigal group. Their style of life was quite different from the countercultural tone of the kids; you felt as if you were having coffee with a faculty couple from Findhorn College. Findhorn, it seemed, embraced all styles and generations; the only style you did not see among the 130 members was the Chippendale-*cum*-doily of an East End séance.

After lunch that day John took a small group of us in a van for an outing to a Benedictine priory, Pluscarden. The weather was perfect for such an outing, for although it was October and the leaves had turned, the Highlands were having a warm flush of what we would call Indian summer. With an RAF base to the south of it, Findhorn was not blessed with a prospect of trees, so the drive into the surrounding hills and valleys and beaches showed just how fine was the landscape a short distance from the trailer camp. Pluscarden was in a very wooded valley and seemed quite happy to share its scenery with Findhorn. Unorthodox as Findhorn was, it seemed it was still on good terms with the monks and even performed concerts with its string quartet at the priory. As an old Roman Catholic, I found this rather hard to believe. Here was a community in which the leaders could talk to the little people, sprites, elves, devas, sons of

God, and God Himself, a community which spoke of extraterrestrial links with space and intraterrestrial links with plants; in short, a community of heretics who should have been huddling together Amish-style to await the end of the world and the judgment of the fallen, but instead were going around singing, working, and gardening on friendly terms with everyone—even the One True Holy Catholic and Apostolic Church!

Findhorn wanted to be on good terms with the Church because the priory, Findhorn, and Cluny Hill expressed a triangle of the ancient "power points" in the area. And just what a power point was I was to learn from David the next morning.

It seems that one of the things that most impressed Peter when I walked into his office was that I had come to Britain only to go to Lindisfarne and Findhorn. While I was at Lindisfarne, a small group was just returning from Iona. The purpose of their journey was to reawaken the power and spirit of Iona for the coming historical moment.

What meets the eye at Findhorn has very little to do with what is going on inside; the cluster of caravans and bungalows would have to be transformed into a science fiction movie set if the outer forms were to be brought into line with Findhorn's visions of cosmic energy. Rather than viewing consciousness as distinct from matter, the people at Findhorn regard matter as a condensation of consciousness. Thus everything is open to consciousness, everything has its own pitch of vibratory resonance. You can commune with plants or spirits of nature if you know how to pitch your consciousness at the same vibratory level. What separates beings in the universe is not space but consciousness. This view of nature seems to be the natural one, for it is a part of our universal folk heritage, Celtic or Hopi; but in the modern era it has been remythologized into the imagery of science fiction. A particular work of science fiction which is very close to the world view of Findhorn is the trilogy of C. S. Lewis. When Ransom is on Mars, a very learned "sorn" tries to give him a lesson about what the universe is really like.

'Start from where we are, Small One. The swiftest thing that touches our senses is light. We do not truly see light, we only see the slower things lit by it, so that for us light is on the edge— the last thing we know before things become too swift for us. But the body of an *eldil* is a movement swift as light; you may say its body is made of light, but not of that which is light for the *eldil*. His "light" is a swifter movement which for us is nothing at all; and what we call light is for him a thing like water, a visible thing, a thing he can touch and bathe in—even a dark thing when not illuminated by the swifter. And what we call firm things—flesh and earth—seem to him thinner, and harder to see, than our light, and more like clouds, and nearly nothing. To us the *eldil* is a thin, half-real body that can go through walls and rocks: to himself he goes through them because he is solid and firm and they are like cloud. And what is true light to him fills the heaven, so that he will plunge into the rays of the sun to refresh from it, is to us the black nothing in the sky at night. These things are not strange, Small One, though they are beyond our senses. But it is strange that the *eldila* never visit Thulcandra [Earth].'

'Of that I am not certain,' said Ransom. It had dawned on him that the recurrent human tradition of bright, elusive people some- times appearing on the Earth—*albs, devas,* and the like—might after all have another explanation than the anthropologists had yet given. True, it would turn the universe rather oddly inside out; but his experiences in the space ship had prepared him for some such operation.[7]

Ransom's experiences in the spaceship prepared him for the turning of reality inside-out, just as the experiences of our astronauts in space prepared them for a similar con- version. Ironically, the expansion of our technology has forced us back to depend, not on the models of reality in civilized writing, but on the archaic models in folklore, fantasy, and science fiction to regain our bearings in infinite space. Men have been insisting for some time that there is more to reality than the light which strikes the eye, and sometimes these men have paid for it. At other times they have been tolerated as creators of entertaining fantasies, and only as fantasts were they able to smuggle their alien models of reality past our customs. But now that our walls are crumbling and all our confident structures of reality are coming apart, it seems that even some scientists and engineers are willing to stand up and be counted as heretics.

Perhaps this is happening now because there is no single ruling elite: the Church has no power over the mind and has become an historical museum filled with more curators than curates; the politicians are too busy to care about anything that does not threaten them immediately; and the ruling leftist intellectuals in the universities, for all their intolerance, have no political base from which to persecute intellectuals outside the university. Because of this pluralization of elites, there is room to search among the cracks in the old reality for air to breathe. Perhaps, as Arthur Koestler has argued,[8] it is because physics is too far-out to be used any longer as a support for the claims of materialism that we are now in an open situation in which so many alternate models of reality are competing with the old mechanistic world picture.

In the days when the normal scientific paradigm[9] was conquering the world, art was a holding action for the spirit; but now that that age is over we seem to be moving away from marking time with works of art to taking our selves seriously again. The edge of the culture has moved beyond reading the science fiction of C. S. Lewis to living in communities like Findhorn. For whatever reason, we are now in a cultural position to move beyond the stages of the Crazies and the Artists to take the ideas of Findhorn seriously. David

Spangler is a man of the third stage, the Savants, but his ideas on energy are indistinguishable from those of Doris Lessing.

The earth is surrounded by its etheric field or vital body which can receive energies flowing through the cosmos or from higher dimensions of vibration and transform these energies into qualities capable of nourishing and vitalizing the denser matter of the physical level. The etheric field, then, is the source of the basic, primal creative energy from which the physical forms are built and from which they are sustained in being.[10]

Although the term "ether" is employed by occultists, it has nothing to do with the ether of nineteenth-century physics, the existence of which was disproved by the Michelson-Morley experiments. This other etheric energy may actually be coming very close to empirical verification. Neuroanatomists have noticed that the electrical paths of the nerves seem to develop before the actual growth and development of the nerve tissue itself.[11] This a priorism of form and pattern over matter absolutely refutes our simplistic notions of mechanism and behaviorism. These proto-neuronal pathways, then, seem to be something like ferromagnetic domains that can give orientation to the energies flowing through them and actually help to build up the nerve tissue that will grow within the domain pathways. It may now very well be the case that the Kirlian photography of the auras and energies flowing out of the bodies of animals and plants (and this work is now being conducted by Dr. Stanley Krippner at the Maimonides Hospital Dream Laboratory in New York and by Dr. Thelma Moss at UCLA) may be images of the etheric energy of the body. According to Spangler, this energy is not "simply located" in the body; the individual body is a prehension of the etheric field around earth.

This field is criss-crossed with lines of power flow, just as a country may be criss-crossed by high-tension electric lines. Seen clairvoyantly, from one level, this network of lines gives the impression of being a web, hence the phrase, "the etheric web of power." . . .

Cosmic Power Points receive energy from universal sources and transform them to planetary requirements. . . . A spiritual teacher may, for example, use the energy of a cosmic power point to establish his own centre of radiance. That is what St. Columba did on Iona, and it was a common practice amongst the ancient adepts and initiates who had knowledge concerning these power centres and the etheric web.

A power centre is a place where the energies of two or more dimensions or patterns of evolution converge and where the barriers between them are thin. This makes it possible for a consciousness on one dimension or within one pattern of evolution to more easily pierce that barrier, contact the other energy and give it access to his area of life.[12]

This etheric web of energy is what the hero of Doris Lessing's *Briefing* sees as he ascends in the crystal. It also seems to be a more literal and concrete rendering of Teilhard de Chardin's "Noosphere," the field of energy and consciousness that encircles the earth. If this energy, when it strikes the individual mind, is transformed into images, then the etheric web may also have a connection with Jung's collective unconscious. If we add Whitehead's philosophy of organism to Lessing, Teilhard, and Jung, we can begin to put all the earlier approximations into one theoretical construction. Whitehead criticized the notion of "simple location" of hunks of matter in containing space and tried to build up a different world picture in which space itself was part of the "prehensive unification" of events in one another. Objects do not sit in space; vibratory events secrete the space around them. In order to deal with a world of serial events in time and simply located objects in space, the brain shuts out all the million signals a second to habituate us to life in a cultural "description of reality."[13] But in times of dream, trance, or meditational state, we escape the dominance of the description to see time, space, and information in new ways; then we discover that our minds are not simply located, that space does not separate mind from mind, and that the collective unconscious is open to us. If we wish to picture the etheric web around the earth in a more contemporary scientific image, we can see it as a superconductor: the power points are domains in which information can be stored; the background of darkness is the magnetic field of earth which tries to wipe out the single-quantum state of the electrons to force all their spins to line up in a single direction and become bound to earth. The superconducting domain can hold information against the Second Law indefinitely; thus when a "sensitive" approaches or stumbles upon a domain or power point, the potential information becomes virtual information in his consciousness and passes over into sound, image, or an intuitive awareness with no sensory base. In ancient cultures the custom was to have the individual sleep in a power point so that the information could bypass the obstructions of the conscious mind to flow into dreams. In the Hypogeum on Malta there is a statue of a sleeping prophetess; tradition says that upon waking she would offer her dream to the priest for interpretation. This archaic heritage of the sacred power of place was resurrected by the romantic poets, especially Wordsworth, who tried to show that there was a special affinity between altered states of consciousness and unusual points in the landscape. If one relates all the power points together, he begins to come up with a psycho-historical map of the culture. In Great Britain, such a map would have among its power points Iona, Lindisfarne, Glastonbury, and Stonehenge.

The psychic mapping of the landscape is a universal feature of human culture. The ancient Irish bard knew the story built into every major feature of the countryside of Ireland; the Arunta in Australia know that as you pass over the land, you pass into the dream-time of the ancestors; the Hopi have a psychic map for all of North America, and the sacred places, like Mount San Francisco, are critical points in their cosmology and history. What the people at Findhorn are doing is creating an archaeology of mind to uncover the ancient world view of Britain. It appears to be a romantic exercise in mythology, but as Lévi-Strauss has pointed out: "Myth is an act of faith in a science yet unborn." Now that thousands of people around the world are working on the anomalies in the old scientific paradigm, it should not take us more than ten or twenty years to create a whole new paradigm of the science of nature and mind. Although we are well out of the phase of the Crazies and well into the phase of the Artists, it may not be long until we are deeply into phase III of the Savants. If we can articulate David Spangler's work on power points with Lessing, Jung, Whitehead, and modern physics, we may have only ten years to wait for the work of a Darwin who will have the patience to build up an entire new paradigm.

In the meantime we have a choice: we may relate to this new material immediately through mysticism and experience the New Age, or we may reject it by invoking the old paradigm of science and wait snobbishly for new men in white laboratory smocks to come along and tell us that it is now all right to believe in power points. But we should remember that if yogis had waited for science to come along and prove the validity of yoga, there would be no yoga existing today to validate in the Menninger and Langley Porter Institutes.

I choose to go ahead and believe in power points and find ways in which to relate more effectively to Teilhard's "Noosphere." Time is running out on this civilization, and if it is the case that an etheric web of power points surrounds nature, or *is* nature, and that this etheric web is the mediation between consciousness on the one hand and matter on the other, then it follows that if enough of us begin plucking the golden strands of that web, the music of nature will be re-tuned and a new harmony created between it and human culture. In religious terms, we can say that there will be "a new heaven and a new earth."

The new heaven and the new earth are forming in your midst and this is the importance of this centre, that it is a magnetic point around which new spheres of consciousness may form. This is why all that has been revealed to you as change is of vital importance, for you must consistently, though at times gradually, align yourselves with the new heaven and the new earth. Then you are under My full protection and My full blessing and shall be increasingly so. As you grow and expand your consciousness, consistently remove from yourselves all of the old. This may be gradual but it must be consistent, for in this way you will remain protected and under My blessing.

Great changes have occurred in kingdoms beyond yours and they also are moving into a new heaven and a new earth. If man does not commune with them, he will be left behind and com-munion will be impossible. All is moving. You are moving not only through space and time but within a dimensional shift; you are moving within Light, Love and Consciousness.

I have been revealed as Truth, as Limitless Love, as Life, and I move steadily towards the consummation of My revelation. For I attract to Me now Lovers from beyond the stars to unite with Me and pour their seed into the earth and transform it, Regents of vast new powers and energies to descend through many centres upon the earth. . . .

I AM now the Life of a new heaven and a new earth. Others must draw upon Me and unite with Me to build its forms. As I have said, be not concerned for your own safety. That which happens to those who have come under different laws and a differ-ent cycle, I cannot influence. They have passed beyond Me in My new revelation, though not beyond Me as I slumber within them. They shall find Me yet, though their way be long and the finding in the future. What they have invoked shall come to them, but it will manifest as beauty and as revelation and as release. . . .

I do not send you forth, who hear My voice, to proclaim the kingdom of the saved and the disaster of the lost. I have stated repeatedly, I AM with all. None are saved. None are lost. There is always only what I AM, but I have revealed Myself in new Life and new Light and new Truth. Those who attune to that will not be saved. They will only be attuned to what I AM in My new revelation. . . . It is My function through this centre to demonstrate what I AM through the medium of group evolution.[14]

It would be considerably easier to consider such a message of revelation in the Bible, the Vedas, or a newly discovered Dead Sea scroll, just as it is easier to take a work of genius when it is safely framed and hanging on the wall of a museum; but when we are asked to take a revelation or a work of art without its cultural frame, we become frightened. Afraid of error or ridicule, it is so much easier to do nothing at all. It is, therefore, very hard to know what to do with David Spangler. He does not look like a Moses or an Elijah, he doesn't come on like Sri Chinmoy; he simply says he closed his eyes, meditated, and received this transmission. Where does it come from—hallucination, imagination, the ether, the collective unconscious, or God? Men have been asking these questions about shamans since the first shaman fell into trance. But David says he is no medium; he does not lose his own self-consciousness, he simply attunes his consciousness to the cosmic wave length—that's all. The message he receives seems to be a variation on a recurring theme, whether it is in Teilhard de Chardin or Arthur C. Clarke's *Childhood's End*, or the organism of a thousand minds of Paolo Soleri, or the Descent of the Supra-Mental of Sri Aurobindo, and the message is that the next stage of human evolution is the emergence of a human collective consciousness. Like a lure-casting fisherman, man seems to cast a fantasy far in front of him and then slowly reel himself into it.

In the twentieth century two quite different steps have been taken toward the creation of a collective consciousness.

The first was the enforced integration of the individual mind with the collectivity of the Total State in Soviet Russia or Maoist China. The second was the unforced lifting of the collective unconscious into culture and was the work of scholars like Freud and Jung, and artists like Blake, Wordsworth, and Kafka. A "spirit of the age" seems to be the most familiar form of collective consciousness, and the rock music of the sixties came close to being so powerful as to uproot a whole generation from one culture to socialize it completely in a new one. But it would seem that before man can merge his consciousness with the race, or with "lovers from beyond the stars," he must be able to merge with the collective unconscious without the destruction of his own individuation. This has been the traditional project of Tibetan Buddhism, as any terrifying Tanka bears witness, but has recently become the subject of Carlos Castaneda's three books on the Mexican way of knowledge. If a man can suffer his ego to endure his self and observe with dispassion the beauties and beasts of the collective unconscious, then he is in a position to be able to endure to see the unique and the universal cross in the collective consciousness of the race, or of the universe in nirbikalpa samadhi.

To be more exact, we should no longer even speak of the collective *un*conscious, for we are now, thanks to Freud and Jung, and all the great artists of the century, more than aware of its existence. The old heresy has become a new orthodoxy; but the Findhorn heresies of the collective consciousness of the race remain free and innocent of "*Nihil obstat.*"

If you are frightened as you consider these ideas, it is a sign that you understand the implications only too well. There *is* a danger to all of this. In the first wave of this evolutionary transformation of man, the rise of the collective unconscious into culture stimulated the political revolutions of Soviet Russia and Nazi Germany. The integration of the individual mind with the collective consciousness must be free, as it is in art or religion; but if art or religion is used to enforce the integration, then we do not have the Mystical Body of Christ but the demonic body of Satan.

It is easy to see the art of the New Age in the music of Stockhausen, but it is harder to see the politics of the New Age. The sixties in America have led us to expect some revolutionary rerun of the Russian or Cuban revolutions. For months before going to Findhorn I had been brooding on the politics of mysticism and how antidemocratic many of the Indian gurus were who spoke of some men being "more highly evolved" than others. From my own study of the rise of the collective unconscious into the culture of revolutionary Ireland, I knew the danger of revolutionary fantasies and the realities of civil war. As I watched the news about Kent State, I could remember Yeats:

> We are closed in, and the key is turned
> On our uncertainty; somewhere
> A man is killed, or a house burned,
> Yet no clear fact to be discerned:
> Come build in the empty house of the stare.

> A barricade of stone or of wood;
> Some fourteen days of civil war;
> Last night they trundled down the road
> That dead young soldier in his blood:
> Come build in the empty house of the stare.

> We had fed the heart on fantasies,
> The heart's grown brutal from the fare;
> More substance in our enmities
> Than in our love; O honey-bees,
> Come build in the empty house of the stare.

My fears should have been quieted by talk with holy men, but even they made me uneasy, and Gopi Krishna seemed rather open in his hopes for a new caste system for the future. With all of this in mind, I had said in an interview that "no one was really talking about the politics of mysticism." David had read that interview and decided to take up the challenge and give a lecture on the topic. He sent off his list of topics and the schedule of the dates for the lectures to the community printer, and on the weekend scheduled for his talk on politics, I drove into Findhorn. It was another one of those synchronicities that made you feel you were moving with others in a dance that a god had choreographed.

Before David gave his lecture, we had occasion to spend a morning in conversation on a long walk down to the shore in Findhorn Bay. I explained my anxiousness at the flood of gurus in the United States: anyone with an itch in his third eye automatically set out his shingle and started a new movement, and from what I could see from Scientology, Arica, and Mind Control, it was all a karmic net in which you got the guru you deserved. Now here I was, leaving the university and trying to start an Association, but I was no guru and didn't want to be set up as one. I had no desire to follow in the footsteps of Oscar Ichazo or John Lilly. And yet it seemed to me that no one but an Initiate should start the Lindisfarne Association; its founder should be a Yogananda or a Rudolf Steiner, for good intentions were simply not enough. David said that anyone who initiates a new cultural movement, be he artist or scientist or mystic, is an initiator, if not an initiate. His words were so simple and straightforward that I saw instantly that I was suffering from a Dr. Strange comic-book vision of the Atlantean Initiate, winging in and out of *lokas*, zapping black magicians with his fire-crystal-laser-ring, dissolving elemental thought-forms with secret mantras, and climbing back onto his throne on top of a pyramid to lay it on his prostrate multitude. If Steiner was right, we had already been through that number. This time, as Tolkien knew, it is time for the little hobbits to carry the ring and for the wizards to stand back. The new religious evolution of man requires not one Great Guru with all the others pranaming on their bellies before him, but a Christ-consciousness in many upright men. What happened to one man before would now happen to Everyman, and that was what all the talk of "the Second Coming" was all about.

David had his own fine sense of irony about these neo-Atlantean fantasies of Initiates; in fact, he had even designed and marketed a spoofing of the occult in a game called "Initiation." David said that he had always felt that any self-respecting Initiate should be able to see auras, but he had never seen an aura in his life. As I listened to David's common sense on the democratic approach to mysticism and the group blending of individual abilities, I began to feel that there was a unique contribution to the New Age that America, not India, could make, and that contribution was politics, the politics of Washington and Jefferson.

In his talk that evening David went on to relate political systems to his theories of the etheric web. He drew another electrical analogy and said that the old etheric web of the previous world cycle was unplugged from its cosmic source; it still had enough energy to last for a while before it ran down completely, but its energy at the moment came from the fact that as any system is unplugged, it receives a last burst of energy. This cultural phenomenon was what I knew as the sunset-effect of movements and institutions. It was now the period of brilliant sunset for the churches, universities, and messianic movements.

Since one of the characteristics of the New Age is collective and group work, with each individual being uplifted, and since the motion and revelation of the Christ is a universal Principle, the day of the strong, dominating individual is past. The pattern for the future is not one of a single person or group leading the rest of humanity into the promised land but of men and women acting through Love and Truth as a leaven with mankind to stimulate and lift the whole, distributing the arising Christ Principle as widely as possible within the race of man.[15]

The old model was hierarchical: Moses on the mountaintop brings down the Tables of the Law to the idolatrous mob which dances before the golden calf of materialism. It was small wonder that when hierarchical Europeans or Asians came to America, they set up a benevolent monarchy. But *Le Roi Soleil* surrounded by his planets is not really an American vision of cosmic order. The nucleus with its orbiting electrons expresses the European model of order; the superconductor in which all the electrons move in many directions but as one single-quantum state expresses the American model of order. The age of the kingly guru surrounded by his worshiping devotees was in its final blazing sunset. Now I understood, after listening to David, why Yogananda, one of the very first gurus to bring classical yoga to the West, had refused to appoint a successor in his ashram, but instead had set up a "Fellowship" in which people could follow a new and more Western path to self-realization.

In the first wave of the romance between East and West, the young Americans who were fleeing the authority of their parents and teachers ran away into the authoritarian arms of the gurus. In many cases, the gurus tried to pass on not only their esoteric techniques for the transformation of consciousness but their exoteric cultural traits as well. The followers had to shave their heads, don saffron robes, and chant in the streets; or, if their master was a Sikh, to wear turbans and white baggy trousers.

After listening to David's talk, I had a much better sense of the role of American culture, with its art and politics, in the coming planetization of mankind. We do not need a violent revolution; we received in the American Revolution all the politics we would need for the New Age; now what we need as we move closer to 1976 is a return to the Jeffersonian democracy of "That government governs best which governs least." We do not need a new civic religion of the world state run by Initiates of Kundalini Yoga; we need to protect spirituality from religion in a secular culture of law in which devotees are protected from the zealous excesses of one another. It is utterly naïve to think that in the near future men will have outgrown the playpen of the American Constitution and will lovingly trust one another. The gurus are tolerant and merely condescending now because they have no political power; but even without power they show full evidence of human frailty and vanity and tend to think that their own yoga is bigger and better than the other guru's. And what is often only a case of mild condescension in the guru becomes in the disciples a fever of zealotry. The true prophet of American mysticism and democratic politics is not Sri Anybodynanda but Walt Whitman:

Bibles may convey, and priests expound, but it is exclusively for the noiseless operation of one's isolated Self, to enter the pure ether of veneration, reach the divine levels, and commune with the unutterable. . . .

It is the fashion among dilletants and fops (perhaps I myself am not guiltless) to decry the whole formulation of the active politics of America, as beyond redemption, and to be carefully kept away from. See you that you do not fall into this error. . . .

. . . this tremendous and dominant play of solely materialistic bearings upon current life in the United States, with the results as already seen, accumulating, and reaching far into the future . . . must either be confronted and met by at least an equally subtle and tremendous force-infusion for purposes of spiritualization, for the pure conscience, for genuine esthetics, and for absolute and primal manliness and womanliness—or else our modern civilization, with all its improvements, is in vain, and we are on the road to a destiny, a status, equivalent, in its real world, to that of the fabled damned.[16]

I had gone to Findhorn thinking that I would find a community where people communed with the devas of plants to grow vegetables out of forces beyond the soil, and I did; but the famous Findhorn garden was for me only a very small part of my interest, for at Findhorn, more than in India, I found the balance between American politics and Eastern mysticism. And looking at the spiritually unbalanced politics of the older Americans and the politically unbalanced mysticism of the younger ones, I knew that was as important as anything I had found around the world. The political impasse I had felt at MIT between bourgeois ideas and Marxist action was coming to an end. And on my last night at Findhorn that ending came to its final point on Cluny Hill.

I had gone to the office to pay for my room and board in order to leave very early the next morning. Since it was the end of the day, Peter was in the office alone, so we talked in that relaxed and quiet mood of reflection that comes at dusk. Then suddenly Peter's face brightened with an idea and he said that he had just received a strong intuitive prompting that he was to take me immediately to the power point of Cluny Hill. We went to the car and drove quickly to the other side of the valley to a wooded hill, parked the car, and walked up, with Peter leading the way in a quickened pace. We hurried as if the time were important, and the time could not have been more perfect, for it was sunset and the whole valley was filled with late sunlight on autumn leaves. Peter explained to me that Cluny Hill was one of the points that Jesus had visited with his uncle, Joseph of Arimathea, and that they had come there from that other cosmic power point, Glastonbury. I accepted the legend and willingly walked with him out of history into myth. As Peter stood me on the point, I heard no words as I had once in Ireland nor saw any images as I had once in Yucatán; I put my eyes up into ajna and, in a normal act of visualization, I made a mandala of the earth as I had before at Lindisfarne. In my visualization I could look over the horizon backward to the places I had been in Europe, Africa, and Asia, and forward to America. Concentrating on the strong points of radiance in Auroville, Iona, Findhorn, and Lindisfarne, I visualized the etheric web of light and knew that there was a new civilization on the earth.

Now I could go back to America, to Whitman's native Long Island, and work to connect a point of light with Findhorn and Auroville. These strands of light, like the proto-neuronal pathways in the body, would then attract physical matter and energies to them so that the light could become embodied in a new college for a new culture. To work to transform America without these energies was as hopeless as trying to power a new house with wires of total rubber; mere political action, no matter how well-meaning, would only insulate society from the very cultural forces it needed to survive and evolve. On the top of Cluny Hill I could envision what the Lindisfarne Association would have to be all about. David was right: it was wrong to wait to initiate this work until I was some Initiate who could walk on water; there was plenty of ground to cover before I even came to the water's edge. The work was not to be a guru opening up yet another ashram in America, but to be a college teacher working to separate the authority of culture from the power of the state in the universities, to formulate a new meditational definition of the consciousness of the educated man, and with this definition to re-vision art, science, and religion toward the transformation of culture in America.

Early the next morning I left for the States, and as I flew over the Atlantic, I saw that there could not have been any short cut; the long way round was the necessary distance from Toronto to New York. Back in Manhattan, it was clear that I was a long way from Findhorn and Auroville; as the financial capital of industrial civilization, New York was the dead center of the present. It was one of those days when the sky was a sulphurous yellow and the roads cluttered with the wrecks of cars from a civilization so advanced toward entropy that it no longer had the energy to take the junk off the roads. As I drove south past the refineries of New Jersey that so expressed what industrial civilization was all about, I could see why some kind of violent apocalypse would come. For those who lock all their psychic energy into dying forms and rigidly resist the pulse of life, there is only death and the denial of death in greed. For those who cannot let go, apocalypse comes to deliver them violently. The refineries of New Jersey and the offices of Manhattan are just such an environment of death and greed.

One morning I awoke to the reality of New York with the sound of trucks and the overturning of garbage cans, and I remembered that at dawn in Srinigar I awoke to the sound of Moslems singing their morning prayers. It was still dark, so the music was close to silence; but the old narrow streets began to widen with the sound of God, and I knew that it would not be long before the light followed.

Acknowledgment

I would like to express my thanks to all the people who took time away from their work to help me with mine: Ian Baldwin, Jr., Karl Basedow, Peter Caddy, Gene Fairly, Richard Falk, Henry Grunwald, Werner Heisenberg, Ivan Illich, Gene Kieffer, Gopi Krishna, Doris Lessing, Dennis Meadows, Edgar Mitchell, Jacob Needleman, Aurelio Peccei, David Spangler, Russell Schweikart, Paolo Soleri, C. F. von Weizsäcker, and John Wilhelm.

To my friend and colleague at the Lindisfarne Association, Robin van Löben Sels, I wish to express my deepest gratitude for all her help with the ideas and experiences of the book while it was in the talking stage, and for all her literary suggestions for revising the manuscript.

To my wife, Gail, I would like to express my deepest gratitude, not merely for the intellectual and editorial help she has contributed to this book and all the books and articles, but for the emotional and spiritual help in a transformative year that involved quitting my job, uprooting my family, establishing Lindisfarne, taking a journey of more than forty thousand miles, and writing this book.

A Note on the Lindisfarne Association

The idea of the Lindisfarne Association began to take shape during 1970 and became a physical reality in 1973 in Southampton, Long Island. It represents a first step in the decentralization of institutional education in America. In the conviction that the new planetary culture was not being expressed by the public school systems and large bureaucratic universities, Lindisfarne was set up as an educational community in which people of all ages could work and study together in new forms of growth and transformation.

The new culture is described as planetary rather than international because the latter suggests an organization of political structures and national cultures. Planetary culture is best defined in terms of anomalies, for anomalies express the limits to the categories of the old reality. Planetary culture is neither world-denying mysticism nor world-destroying materialism; it is a Pythagorean synthesis of science, art, and religion; it is economics *and* ecstasy, preindustrial magic *and* postindustrial technology, myth *and* history: in short, it is an embodiment of transcendence.

The thesis of Lindisfarne is that cultural transformations are more effective in bettering the condition of men than violent revolutions: the Crusades were failures, but the Renaissance was a success. The Lindisfarne Association is designed to be a vehicle of the new planetary Renaissance and not a political tool for the attackers or defenders of industrial society. Like the first Lindisfarne of A.D. 635, the Association is more of a cultural strategy than a permanent institution.

What is visible now in society in the form of institutions is the past; what is invisible now to society but experienced by individuals in consciousness is the planetary culture of the immediate future. The doorway to this new universal culture is neither the charismatic individual nor the routine institution (civilization has been going around in those Weberian cycles for some time); it is the spiritual community or fellowship of fully individuated men and women who look around and recognize that what is unique to them is part of a universal transformation in which human cultural evolution is becoming conscious.

Because Lindisfarne is not training people for functions in industrial society, but is fostering the growth of a new culture, it is concerned with Teilhard de Chardin's "Noosphere" in a very literal way. The way to effect the most profound cultural transformation is not to expend one's energies in attacking institutions or industrial society as a whole, but to surround society with a new field of consciousness. In the whole psychic orchestration of consciousness in the Noosphere, the very young and the very old are as important as the generation in power. One group may be *in* power, but all are *in* consciousness; and it is consciousness which creates culture. A child is not worried about being trained for a job; he delights in learning as a puppy delights in running. Lindisfarne is a place where a seven-year-old girl and a sixty-eight-year-old woman can take a class together in Tai Chi, and then have a chat about it afterward.

But the young and the old are not the only ones who are not interested in job-training. Successful people in middle age who are bored with "making it" in careers also become interested in "how to be" rather than in merely "what to do." For them, Lindisfarne becomes a place where they can rethink the changing directions of their lives. For graduate students, Lindisfarne is a place of study for a year or so before committing themselves to the system of professionalization contained in doctoral candidacy. For many undergraduates and high school students, Lindisfarne may be an appropriate cultural vehicle only after a period of healthy creative expansion in cultural vehicles closer to the Israeli kibbutz or the Chinese commune.

When one considers the age groups involved in Lindisfarne, he can see that it is not a college. When one considers the emphasis placed on solitude, privacy, individual creativity, and meditation, he can see that it is not a countercultural commune. Lindisfarne is an educational community rooted in spiritual self-discipline; and in a community, education takes place not so much in terms of techniques as in patterns of culture.

In industrial culture, the body was too often an embarrassment or an instrument for competition and aggression. In planetary culture, the body is once again recognized to be a field of energy having more than three dimensions. In some dimensions, the body is located as matter; in others, as etheric radiation; and in still others, as pure consciousness, satchitananda. At Lindisfarne, the energization of the body is the basis for all the other levels of education. Today there are many fads and fashions in energization, but we feel that the classical techniques are the best, and so we work with the "prana" of Hatha Yoga and the "Chi" of Tai Chi Chuan.

After the work with the physical body comes the work with the psychic body. Industrial culture was one in which the unconscious was savagely repressed, which is a case that has been argued by a constellation of geniuses from Blake and Wordsworth to Lawrence, Freud, and Jung. As we open ourselves to the visualization of new energies within the body at Lindisfarne, so do we open ourselves to the visual energies of dreams; and as the energies begin to flow through the physical and psychic bodies, the transformation begins. There are many fads and fashions in psychology, but Lindisfarne restricts itself to a dream workshop conducted along the lines of thought of Jungian Analytical Psychology.

Just as institutions are being surrounded by the Noosphere of planetary culture, so the intellect is being surrounded by a larger, supramental consciousness. This consciousness is experienced through meditation, and at Lindisfarne the techniques of meditation of the great universal religions are affirmed. Lindisfarne does not offer *a* teaching; it does offer its center to Christians, Jews, Moslems, Buddhists, and Hindus. One student may be following Transcendental Meditation, another a Sufi technique, while a third may be practicing the *Lectura Divina* of the Benedictines.

There are many religious centers today which are concerned with bringing people of all faiths and contemplative practices together, and so Lindisfarne is not unique in this. Lindisfarne, however, is unique in its attempt to integrate art, science, and religion in a new definition of the educated man. Just as the traditional liberal arts college offers "the Great Books" as the foundation for a person's professional training and development, so Lindisfarne offers the great spiritual disciplines for the transformation of consciousness as the foundation for a person's existence in the new planetary culture. Directly concerned with the interface between esoteric and exoteric forms of thought, Lindisfarne offers seminars in science and the humanities by scholars who are rooted in daily meditational practice.

It is expected that the average resident will stay at Lindisfarne for a year, though he is free to enroll for only one of the annual four sessions. The Association grants no credits, degrees, diplomas, or certificates of residence. The standards for achievement are the natural ones of individuals working toward their own self-mastery; there are no other means of examination or evaluation. Lindisfarne does not wish to compromise its freedom by being turned into a subcontractor for the giants in the education industry; therefore, it does not administer tests or means of credit evaluation for other institutions. The Association keeps no record of a resident's stay at Lindisfarne, nor endorses any application to another institution. The decision to award credits for study at Lindisfarne must be a personal decision between the resident and those institutions interested in the awarding of credits.

The process of education at Lindisfarne can be expressed in stages. First, we come to know our bodies as matter; then we discover them to be fields of energy. As the energy flows through us, we turn ourselves inside out and see the energy-flow in the primordial alphabet of symbols of our dreams. Then, in meditation, we see that we are not, as Whitehead would say, "simply located" in space-time as a mass of energy or a theater of dreams. With the discovery of the higher levels of consciousness, we, paradoxically, come out of meditational solitude into the Noosphere, in which we all flow like electrons in a superconducting, single-quantum state. As in the conclusion to the Zen ox-herding pictures, we return to the city of man with "bliss-bestowing hands" and realize that contained in our private discovery of "how to be" is a new and marvelously unpredictable, cultural discovery of "what to do."

Notes

TWO Walking Out On the University

1. Frances L. Ilg, M.D., and Louise Bates Ames, Ph.D., *Child Behavior*, Gesell Institute (New York, 1955), p. 12.

"We have here started this summary of cycles of behavior at two years of age, but actually it could have been begun in infancy, when the same kinds of alternation of ingoing and outgoing periods, periods of equilibrium and disequilibrium, do occur. . . . From one to two years, the intervals of change lengthen to three months, and from two years to seven years, to six months. From seven to ten years (and on to sixteen years) these salient changes appear to take place less frequently—at about yearly intervals. It is probable that this spiral of growth slows down even further during the twenties and thirties, but it seems quite possible that predictable changes are continuing to take place, though less clearly defined, during these and the succeeding years and probably throughout human life's span."

THREE. The Individual as Institution

1. Paolo Soleri, *Arcology: The City in the Image of Man* (Cambridge, 1969).
2. A. F. C. Wallace, "Revitalization Movements," *American Anthropologist*, April, 1956.
3. Paolo Soleri, *The Bridge Between Matter and Spirit Is Matter Becoming Spirit* (New York, 1973), p. 128.
4. *Ibid.*, p.8. "It is the furnace of the sun" is taken from the first draft.

5. *Ibid.*, p. 252.
6. Donella H. Meadows, Dennis Meadows, Jørgens Randers, William Behrens III, *The Limits to Growth: A Report of the Club of Rome's Project on the Predicament of Mankind* (New York, 1972).
7. Pierre Teilhard de Chardin, *The Future of Man* (New York, 1964), pp. 130, 132.
8. Paolo Soleri, *Arcology*, p. 12.
9. Robert Fogelson, *Fragmented Metropolis: Los Angeles, 1850–1930* (Cambridge, 1968).
10. Marshall McLuhan, "Interview," *Playboy*, March, 1969.
11. Aurelio Peccei, *The Chasm Ahead* (New York, 1969).
12. Christopher Tugendhat, *The Multinationals* (New York, 1972), p. 220.
13. Ivan Illich, *Deschooling Society* (New York, 1971).
14. Paolo Soleri, *Arcology*, p. 109.
15. Sri Aurobindo and the Mother, *The Destiny of Man* (Pondicherry, India, 1969), p. 119.
16. Jacob Needleman, *The New Religions* (New York, 1970).
17. Paolo Soleri, "Religion as Simulation," p. 17, unpublished paper.

FOUR.   The World State and the Shadow of H. G. Wells

1. Werner Heisenberg, *Physics and Beyond: Encounters and Conversations* (New York, 1971), p. 158.
2. Lovat Dickson, *H. G. Wells: His Turbulent Life and Times* (London, 1972), p. 269.
3. Dennis Livingston, "Science Fiction Models of Future World Order Systems," *International Organization*, XXV, No. 2, 1971, 254–270.
4. W. Warren Wagar, *H. G. Wells and the World State* (New Haven, 1961).
5. Donella H. Meadows *et al.*, *op. cit.*
6. W. Warren Wagar, *Building the City of Man: Outlines of a World Civilization* (New York, 1971), p. 54.
7. *Ibid.*, p. 36.
8. *Ibid.*, p. 59.
9. *Ibid.*, p. 66.
10. *Ibid.*, p. 71.
11. Arnold Toynbee, *Surviving the Future* (New York, 1971), pp. 81, 113–114.
12. W. Warren Wagar, *Building the City of Man*, p. 112.
13. Robert Jungk, *Brighter Than a Thousand Suns* (New York, 1958), pp. 96, 105.
14. Werner Heisenberg, *op. cit.*, p. 151.
15. I realize that many people doubt Weizsäcker's version of his wartime activities and are convinced that he was actively working with

the Nazis to build an atom bomb. In Weizsäcker's version, he suggested to Heisenberg that he tell Bohr that there was no danger of the Germans' building an atom bomb, and when Heisenberg did this, Bohr misunderstood. According to the other version, Bohr thought that Heisenberg was trying to suggest that the Allies not build a bomb so that his Germany would not be incinerated. Unfortunately, history is as complicated as a Pirandello play, and since we have only memories of unrecorded conversations to go by, there seems little hope of ever knowing the truth. At all events, the material from Jungk, Weizsäcker, and Heisenberg is consistent. Ultimately, opinions in this historical matter do not rest upon evidence, but on the belief structures of the researcher: one either believes that Heisenberg was motivated to adopt Max Planck's strategy for the survival of German science, or he does not. For obvious historical reasons, many Dutch and Jewish scientists do not believe the story as it is presented in Jungk. I simply do not know the truth, and in the absence of proof, I am giving Heisenberg and Weizsäcker the benefit of the doubt.

16. Donella H. Meadows, *et al., op. cit.*
17. Jay Forrester, *Urban Dynamics* (Cambridge, 1969).
18. Harvey A. Averch and Robert A. Levine, "Two Models of the Urban Crisis: An Analytical Essay on Banfield and Forrester," The RAND Corporation, RM-6366-RC, September, 1970.

    "Forrester's work does not suffer from logical inconsistencies, nor is its use of evidence faulty; rather it floats free of any empirical evidence. Every structural relation and number in the model is an assumed one without any justification based on data from the real world."
19. Lovat Dickson, *op. cit.*, p. 123.
20. Aurelio Peccei, "The Great Doom Debate," conference reprinted from *The Observer*, no date.
21. Aurelio Peccei, *The Chasm Ahead* (New York, 1969).
22. Press release on the history of the Club of Rome, p. 4.
23. Donella H. Meadows *et al., op. cit.*, p. 190.

FIVE. Of Physics and Tantra Yoga

1. Gopi Krishna, *The Biological Basis of Religion and Genius* (New York, 1972).
2. Werner Heisenberg, *op. cit.*, p. 11.
3. Erwin Schrödinger, *My View of the World* (London, 1964).
4. Werner Heisenberg, "The Representation of Nature in Contemporary Physics" in *Symbolism in Religion and Literature*, ed. Rollo May (New York, 1960), p. 209.
5. A. N. Whitehead, *Science and the Modern World* (New York, 1967), p. 37.

6. C. F. von Weizsäcker, "Introduction" to Gopi Krishna, *The Biological Basis of Religion and Genius*, p. 41.
7. *The Upanishads*, trans. F. Max Mueller, Volume II (New York, 1962), p. 88.
8. René Descartes, *Selections*, ed. R. M. Eaton (New York, 1927), p. 145.
9. André Leroi-Gourhan, *Treasures of Prehistoric Art* (New York, 1967).
10. C. F. von Weizsäcker, *loc. cit.*, p. 30.
11. *Ibid*, p. 42.
12. Gopi Krishna, *Kundalini: The Evolutionary Energy in Man* (Berkeley, 1971).
13. Satprem, *Sri Aurobindo or the Adventure of Consciousness* (Pondicherry, India, 1970), p. 59.
14. See Doris Lessing's *Four-Gated City* (New York, 1967) and the short story, "Each Other," in *A Man and Two Women* (New York, 1963).
15. C. G. Jung, *Aion* (Princeton, 1959), p. 211.
16. See Mircea Eliade, *The Two and the One* (New York, 1969).
17. Robert Keith Wallace and Herbert Benson, "The Physiology of Meditation," *Scientific American*, February, 1972, pp. 84–92. Gopi Krishna insists that the erotic fluids of women flow into the spinal column in the same manner as the reversed seminal fluid of men who experience the elevation of kundalini. Personally, I do not think this is the case. The sexual fluids in the vagina are not analogous to the seminal fluids. If men use the prana involved in seminal production, then women would have to use the enormous prana involved in the production of the ovum and the endometrial lining of the womb. Man, as all his countless plays, poems, and novels express, is torn apart between the polarities of spirituality and sexuality. As Yeats expresses it in *A Full Moon in March*:

> SECOND ATTENDANT: I cannot face that emblem of the moon
> Nor eyelids that the unmixed heavens dart,
> Nor stand upon my feet, so great a fright
> Descends upon my savage, sunlit heart.
> What can she lack whose emblem is the moon?
> FIRST ATTENDANT: But desecration and the lover's night.

In terms of Tantra Yoga, we can say that men are pulled apart between the second and the sixth chakra, the sexual and the psychic; in a state of perpetual contradiction and unrest, men move and are dynamically striving after sexual satisfaction and spiritual transfiguration of their fierce drives. Male sexuality is rooted in objects and actions. Women's sexuality is rooted in being and states of feeling; their arousal does not come from the genital fixations of pornography but from the deepest sexual emanations and aura of the lover. In terms of Tantra Yoga, we can say that the polarities of female sexuality are between the third and the fourth chakras, between the navel and the heart. Quite literally, woman's sexuality is at a higher level than man's. Focused on the navel, the woman is literally at the center of the universe *when* she is in her own center. At its best, this means that woman has no place she has to get to; at its worst, it means that woman can be nailed through the navel into time, so that locked into the kitchen she can make fun of all the silly toys of the little men of civilization. As I have argued before, one's unique excellence is also his tragic flaw; *areté* equals *hamartia*. When women are not in their center, focused on the life-giving qualities of the navel and the emotional feelings of the heart, they become the other image of the sustaining Mother, Kali the Destroyer. Whether she is Kali, Clytaemnestra, Medea, Lady Macbeth, or just a shrill harpie from Women's Gay Liberation, she expresses the violent contradictions between life and death, womb and tomb. At all events, the arousal of kundalini in women is, I believe, much more complicated than Gopi Krishna admits. I shall try to go into this in greater detail in a forthcoming book.

18. See Sri Aurobindo, *The Mind of Light* (New York, 1971), p. 68.
19. Gopi Krishna, *The Secret of Yoga* (New York, 1972), p. 74.
20. Gopi Krishna, *The Biological Basis of Religion and Genius*, p. 115.
21. Sri Aurobindo and the Mother, "On Democracy and Socialism," pamphlet, Sri Aurobindo Ashram, Pondicherry, India, 1972, p. 9.
22. In Robert Jungk, *op. cit.*, p. 81.

SIX. Planetary Mythologies

1. *The New Science of Giambattista Vico*, ed., T. Bergin and M. Fisch (Ithaca, 1970), p. 27.
2. S. N. Kramer, *The Sumerians: Their History, Culture, and Character* (Chicago, 1963).
3. Eric Hobsbawm, *The Age of Revolution: 1789–1848* (New York, 1962), p. 310.
4. Glyn Daniel, *The Idea of Prehistory* (New York, 1962), p. 32.
5. Uwe Essmann and Herman Träuble, "The Magnetic Structure of Superconductors," *Scientific American*, March, 1971, p. 75. See also Barry Commoner, *Science and Survival* (New York, 1966), p. 42.
6. Edmund Leach, *Genesis as Myth* (London, 1966).
7. Erich von Däniken, *Chariots of the Gods?* (London, 1969).
8. *The Urantia Book* (Chicago, 1955).

9. Doris Lessing, *Briefing for a Descent into Hell* (London, 1971).
10. Edouard Schuré, *From Sphinx to Christ: An Occult History* (New York, 1970).
11. Kenneth Boulding, *The Meaning of the Twentieth Century: The Great Transition* (New York, 1964), p. 155.
12. Sri Aurobindo, *The Destiny of Man* (Pondicherry, India, 1969), p. 18.
13. Gopi Krishna, *The Biological Basis of Religion and Genius*, p. vii.
14. Pierre Teilhard de Chardin, *op. cit.*, p. 127.
15. Joel de Rosnay, "Evolution and Time," *Main Currents in Modern Thought*, December, 1970, pp. 35–47.
16. Sri Aurobindo, *The Mind of Light*, p. 76.
17. Darcy Ribeiro, *The Civilizational Process* (New York, 1968).

SEVEN. To Findhorn and Lindisfarne

1. Henry Kelsey, *St. Aidan and St. Cuthbert* (Berwick on Tweed, no date), p. 23.
2. *Ibid.*
3. Máire and Liam De Paor, *Early Christian Ireland* (London, 1958), p. 49.
4. Jacob Needleman, *op. cit.*, p. 16.
5. *Ibid.*, p. 202.
6. Henry Kelsey, *op. cit.*, p. 23.
7. C. S. Lewis, *Out of the Silent Planet* (New York, 1965), p. 94.
8. Arthur Koestler, *The Roots of Coincidence* (New York, 1972), p. 50.
9. T. S. Kuhn, *The Structure of Scientific Revolutions* (Chicago, 1962).
10. David Spangler, "The Iona Report" (Findhorn, 1972), p. 1.
11. Leonard Ravitz, "Studies of Man in the Life Field," *Main Currents in Modern Thought*, September, 1962, pp. 13–23.
12. David Spangler, *loc. cit.*
13. Carlos Castaneda, *Journey to Ixtlan* (New York, 1972), p. 8.
14. David Spangler, *Revelation: The Birth of a New Age* (Findhorn, 1971), pp. 110, 121.
15. *Ibid.*, p. 71.
16. Walt Whitman, *Leaves of Grass and Selected Prose*, ed., John Kouwenhoven (New York, 1950), pp. 491, 514.

Index

About the Author

William Irwin Thompson was born in Chicago in 1938, but spent most of his early life in California. He attended Pomona College, where he studied philosophy and anthropology, and Cornell University, where he studied literature and history, and received his Ph.D. in 1966. He has held Woodrow Wilson and Old Dominion fellowships and has taught in various fields of the humanities at Cornell, MIT, Syracuse, and York University in Toronto. In 1973 he became the founding director of a new educational and religious center, The Lindisfarne Association, in Southampton, New York (P.O. Box 1395, Southampton 11968). Mr. Thompson is also the author of *The Imagination of an Insurrection: Dublin, Easter 1916* (1967); and *At the Edge of History* (1971).